BEING EMPLOYABLE

AN INITIATIVE BY JJ SCHOOL OF EMPLOYABILITY

All profits from sale of this book go to
Shree Rajendra Honeycomb Charitable Trust

FOREWORD BY JOGESH JAIN

First Published in August 2020

Published By:
bizHQ
An imprint of Kalon Maple Publishing
+91 9665 609 444

ISBN: 9798674452386
Price: ₹199

Layout Design:
Mrunaal Gawhande

Cover Design:
Dhanashree Pimputkar

Distributed by:

Paperback: amazon.com, amazon.in, flipkart, kalonmaplepublishing.com
Pothi.com
E-Book: amazon.in/com, apple (ibooks stores in 51 countries), barnes &
noble (us and uk), scribd, kobo, and blio, overdrive (world's largest
library ebook platform serving 20,000 + libraries), baker & taylor axis
360, tolino, gardners, Google Play Books, bibliotheca cloud library (3,000 public
libraries) and odilo

CONTENTS

AN INITIATIVE BY JJ SCHOOL OF EMPLOYABILITY

FOREWORD BY

JOGESH JAIN

What is the definition of "Being Employable" in today's time? Traditionally, till the pre-COVID era, employability was all about having 'one' job, being hardworking and dedicated to that job and earning a salary from that job, paying EMIs, bills from that salary, going to bed and doing the same thing all over again, the next day.

My purpose pre-COVID was to help those people who had lost their jobs or were on the verge of losing their jobs, get their "dream job". Till that time, I knew there were plenty of jobs and mostly the candidates were not trained on finding their dream job and that's where I came in.

But COVID has forever changed the definition of employability in the present scenario. As much as I want to say that there are many jobs out there, the truth is there just aren't enough jobs for all the 12 crore people who have just lost their jobs and entered into the market unprepared and without much choice of their own.

What happens to all these candidates now who have EMIs to pay, who have bills to pay, school fees to pay, groceries to buy and elders to take care of.

And that's where the new definition of 'Employability' comes in. 'Being Employable' should not or cannot just be about 'One' Job, 'One Source of Income' and 'One Boss'. We as candidates need to evolve.

Just like a 'phone' evolved into a 'smartphone', we need to evolve from being 'employees' who depend on employers for our income to becoming 'Gigsters' while being employed, who also know how to generate multiple income sources and can serve multiple clients on their own, completely bypassing our employers.

We could stay being loyal to our organizations but will the organization stay loyal to us if they don't get projects, if they don't get revenue or if they don't get new clients? No! They would be the first ones to let us go, with a cake and a few gifts.

Aren't we more responsible towards our family members, towards our own growth as an individual and as a professional than stay enslaved to an employer, who turns their wheels away from us as the going gets tough?

Therefore, I am changing the definition of becoming employable to not only having a job but adding more sources of income to our portfolio based on our skillset, our experience, our ability to work hard and solely dependent on our brain powers.

As time changes, we need to change with time, else become extinct like the Nokia Phone, the cassette tapes, the DVD players and the boombox.

Stay Awake and Keep Evolving.

Jogesh Jain
Founder of JJ School of Employability and MakingIndiaEmployable.com

NEHA TRIPATHI

Neha Tripathi is the Founder Host of Neha Tripathi Talk Show and BAU Head - Women Empowerment, AntWak. She is a Professional Speaker and an Employability Mentor for Women on a Career Break. An Ex-Investment Banker with a decade of Corporate Experience, now a Startup Enthusiast. She is now on a mission to bring a positive shift in % of Women's Leadership Positions.

HER VICTORIOUS RELAUNCH

Year 2018. This was the year when I was receiving so much from life. Everything was falling in my perfect definition of abundance. The same year also turned out to be the kickoff journey of my entrepreneurship, but with a little hiccup.

I have always believed that every experience of my life has refined me to be a step ahead of who I was a previous day. During this phase I was stepping into a new life. 2018 was the year I tied the knot and decided to relocate to a different city. I am a crazy traveler. I love exploring mountains and losing myself in the arms of Nature. Delhi made me a professional woman and fulfilled all my dreams to hug mountains whenever I wanted. After a decade, I wanted to explore more and henceforth decided to relocate to a new city.

The entire process took three months. I was finally in Bangalore. I should have been happy. Instead I found something big missing from my life. Shifting from a place where I had my family, where I had spent my childhood and where all my college friends lived, to a place where local language was in itself alien to me. Or I would say, I was an alien here. I was in a forced solitude. For straight 12 hours (9AM to 9PM) I was all by myself for 5 days a week.

I was still contemplating on my plans on whether to go back to my corporate job, or to enjoy my current phase or work on my childhood dream to start my business. Cooking was something which I hated to my core. But my house served as my biggest strength. The wide-open space, access to natural light all day long, gave me immense strength. I started gardening. It gave me peace to settle down and reflect on the immense opportunities that I could create. I used to keep my front door open, sit on my coffee table with my laptop, and find solutions to my lost ways.

And after a lot of introspection, thinking, and many conversations with myself in solitude, I came up with the following 21 authentic strategies that I applied and got million dollar worth of clarity from.

21 ways to bounce back from your career break

1. Career Break is your strength. Yes, it is. Acceptance and acknowledgement are the first step. It is time for you to take a pause and reflect back to your life. Ask some tough questions about your future. Question your present because, what you are currently doing, thinking and planning today becomes your future. A temporary fix is a temporary source to happiness. So, take it slow and then come back with a clear lifelong vision.

2. Sabotage your self-doubt before it sabotages your existence in your head. It is easier said than done. It takes courage to do that. But you do not have an option.

3. Social media is a boon if you allow it to serve you. It is a monster if you fall prey to it and lose track of your precious time.

4. "An undivided attention and a focused mind", this is a secret ingredient for you to dream and achieve big.

5. Engage actively with communities of your niche. A fully nurtured community can be your biggest asset. You need to leverage that community. Start with attending Summits, Conferences, Local communities, Business Events. Once you start, you will get better clarity on what kind of people you admire and aspire to become.

6. Network is your net worth. This is actually an understatement. Your network is far beyond your imagination. It is an access to your dreamland, Dream Company, dream life and much more. Do not underestimate the power of your network. Keep churning your network. Redefine your network. Lastly, do not operate from the mindset of a victim. Operate in your network from the mindset of power and wisdom. The real magic happens there.

7. Give strict timelines to your priority. As a lady, you wear different hats. If you fail to acknowledge the value of each hat, you might fail in the long run irrespective of everything that you have done. One of the hats is your Aspirations. You might not want to regret giving up on your dreams on your final day on this earth.

8. Ask for help. Yes, reach out to people who can support you in your journey. I agree not everyone does that. But this is the right time to also face that not everyone is for you.

9. Quit 100 times a day. Oh yes, I did that. Ha-ha. I literally had quit countless times in a day. I felt like no matter how much effort I put; it just is not giving me results. And I would quit. But you know where the beauty is. It is when you start your next day with deeper grit. It is when you do not allow a single day or a week's result define your destiny. It is YOU who define it. PERIOD!!

10. Upgrade Yourself. You are losing out on time. Why would someone hire a woman on a sabbatical? If you answer that question honestly to yourself, I guess I do not need to explain this one.

11. Stop self-victimizing yourself. Honestly, I lose all my respect for anyone who blames the world for who they are today. The sooner you take the responsibility, better are the chances for you to turn around your story.

12. Employer or Employee, whatever is your call, go for it. Excel in your field. There is no easy way, everyone hustles to figure out. In fact the need of an hour is to operate from an Entrepreneurial Leader Mindset. The secret is simple, you know your space better than anyone who might think they know.

13. Why should a resume of a woman on a career break should be shortlisted? This question in itself has immense power. It will bring you in an action mode if you just understand the authenticity of it.

14. Build up on your Personal Brand. Your personal expertise is everything that the world is looking out for. Honestly, I built my community and gave my first talk in a college during my sabbatical. I knew my strengths and showcased it in the best possible way.

15. I always believed that I am the source. I am the source of what I want to manifest in life. I knew I was employable. The only missing link was I was not Employed. And within 6 months I decided to be an Employer and never succumb to any career hiccups in future.

16. Execution gives the ultimate results. Do not be a door to door visitor. Attending webinars, taking courses, reading books, helps only when you execute. Until then nothing on this earth might save you.

17. Get a professional Mentor who can actually give you a perspective. The lens which will be used by a third person will be completely different from your family and friends. Unbiased Mirror reflection, trust me, is something that you badly need.

18. Invest in your personal and professional expertise. Learn Strategies and tricks to get things done. In this digital world, everything is at the comfort of your space. Your hesitation to invest in yourself can cost you big time, and the outcome is irreparable.

19. Persevere and your world will fall in place. I have seen this since my childhood. I was rebellious (as my father would call me). I was totally okay with the term and in fact proud of the fact that I was rebellious. If I want something, I have to go for it even if it needs fighting with my limiting beliefs.

20. You do not have to fit yourself in the culture-scape. Their definition can be questioned. You can question the frame you do not want to be in. Needs clarity of thoughts, willpower and grit to do it. This is also a reason not everyone can bring a shift in society.

21. Lastly, take this career break as a lesson of your life. Bring awareness in your family, community, society. Your life lessons, mistakes and learnings will serve our young generations. Going back to the diverse hats we wear, here are few additional hats that I decided to wear:

    a. As a mother: When I am raising my (future) girl child with pride, I will speak to her when the right time comes. I will inspire her to be a thought leader, a change maker, someone who challenges the boundaries that define a gender. And will then encourage her to be a role model for the society, encourage her to make independent choices in life and take responsibility for all of them, encourage her to live her life the way she wants. How will I raise my (future) boy.. I am planning to write a book on that. Haha!!

b.   As a Professional: You are a role model. Your journey is inspiring. Look around for young aspiring girls and women in their mid-career. Serve them as a mentor in their life. A mentor you never had. The kind of mentor you wanted for yourself.

c.   As a friend: Volunteer to reach out to your friend on break or who is planning to take a break. If you cannot do anything to change her situation just listen to her. She might only need an unbiased person who can understand her. Who else can be a better listener other than a woman who has navigated through her own sabbatical? And, if you are at a power position who can do something, just do it. Selfless service is the most novel thing on earth that you can do.

d.   As a Woman: Support Women in your Life.

NAGANANDA CHANDRASHEKAR

Nagananda Chandrashekar is a seasoned Engineering professional with Core Competencies in the area of Project Management, Supply Chain Management, Business Management, Manufacturing and Product Development with over 20 years of Industry Experience. His mission is to leverage his expertise to create sustainable, productive and thriving organizations in a globally competitive and humane market.

SERENDIPITY

It was the year 2007; I was working with Tata Automation Ltd (TAL) a subsidiary of Tata Motors. Tata Automation is basically a spin off from Tata Motors which was started as a dedicated entity to cater to the machinery requirements of Tata Motors for their assembly line.

Initially they specialized predominantly in developing SPM's (Special Purpose Machines) for the assembly line. However, as the need grew so also the expertise of Tata Automation grew.

They also started developing material handling equipment's (Conveyors and other associated equipment) for the assembly line and also fluid power systems to provide hydraulic and pneumatic power packs to SPM's and Material Handling equipment.

However, as business grew and the expertise of TAL grew, they became an independent entity and started servicing customers other than Tata Motors. The company also forayed into the development of standard CNC machines for the manufacturing industry.

I was working in the machine tool division of TAL responsible for the design and development of standard machines as well as SPM's. It was a great learning experience for me and it added a lot of valuable experience, skill sets and expertise to my career.

However, with liberalization and the advent of many MNC giants and also many local competitors the growth of the machine tool industry was not significant. Hence, I was contemplating on a job change to a different domain. Though I was doing the job search activity it wasn't a focused effort and I was very casual about it as my own career was doing relatively well at Tata Automation.

It was the first weekend of July 2007, and being a holiday, my colleagues and I had planned to go for a new released hit movie. We had discussed and planned for it on the evening of the working day, and scheduled it for the afternoon of the weekend.

The weekend arrived and as discussed, I called my friends to enquire about what time we would be meeting up at the movie hall and accordingly I would also start.

To my dismay one of the colleagues had fallen sick and the other one had got stuck with some urgent personal work, so it resulted in quenching my excitement and adding fuel to my disappointment.

I languished in that state for about half an hour or so and then coming to terms with the reality I came back to my senses.

It is then I started thinking, what else to do on that day since the planned event had been cancelled. I was not used to buying a newspaper, however, on that day it just casually occurred to me to buy a newspaper.

I thought I will do some reading and kill some time and also in the events section if I find any good musical event happening, I may as well go alone and enjoy it. So, I ended up going to the market and picked up a newspaper and returned to my apartment. I started casually glancing through the newspaper, and I happened to chance upon a walk-in interview happening by L&T.

I just decided to give it a shot. So, I quickly got myself ready, arranged for a couple copies of my resume and my certificates and headed out to the walk-in. Two rounds of technical interviews happened, followed by a HR round and I was told that I will receive feedback within a weeks' time.

Lo and behold a couple of days after the walk-in, the HR executive from L&T called me and told me that I needed to go for a medical test at their designated medical center and if the medical was ok then I was through.

I gave the medicals and kept my fingers crossed and anxiously waited for the result as it took almost a week till the medical report reached the company. So, after a week an email congratulating me that my medical was through and I had been selected and a job offer was made.

The HR executive also called me and told me about my joining date and also the company would make arrangements for my stay temporarily for about a week upon joining at their guest house and I was to find an accommodation in the meantime. My joy knew no bounds. I just couldn't believe that I landed up with a new job offer just by accident.

In a nutshell, a lost opportunity (Newly released Movie) propelled me to an even better opportunity for a Job offer from a premier company like L&T and I spent the next 6 years of my life until 2013 at L&T Powai, Mumbai.

DEEPAK SINGH

Deepak Singh is an entrepreneur who makes people healthier & happier. He is on a mission to "Make India Healthier". He has an MBA from the Indian Institute of Technology (ISM), Dhanbad. His education was followed by nine years in leading multinational companies and four years in the restaurant business.

His life goal is to serve customers with healthy and tasty food options. Starting from a small food cart, he has upgraded his business, which includes a takeaway restaurant today. When not absorbed in his mission, Deepak pursues meditation and self-healing.

PLAN B OF LIFE

I have been an entrepreneur for the last 4 years. The journey has not been easy. It has been full of ups and downs. I have a restaurant that's pretty much shut down for the last 2.5 months because of the COVID situation.

Many people are finding the COVID pandemic extremely difficult. Some are losing their jobs and others are fearing that they might lose their jobs.

But I am seeing light at the end of the tunnel. Instead of cribbing about my restaurant being shut down, I looked for an alternative. A long-lasting alternative that can never get shutdown.

I discovered the way to do business online under the guidance of Jogesh Jain. This is what we should do when life gives us lemons, we should make lemonade.

But this time I am not going to spend my time and energy figuring out my own way to success. I am going to follow Jogesh's route, his blueprint, and build my own business online, as I have firm belief in JJ's value of building a meaningful community.

Traditional mindset says that any business takes years to break even and give monetary results but with this business model which is solely based on working online, giving value to others, reaching a large number of people, results are achieved sooner than later.

But it requires one to learn new concepts, surrender to the process of the Guru and implement and take actions. So, I am not going to enter the swimming pool without knowing how to swim.

Thankfully I have values given by JJ. This model is my light at the end of the tunnel and I will be doing what I have always loved to do, give people value and knowledge in my area of expertise.

As lockdown opens up, my restaurant will also open up but this day and age is not just about Plan A - A single source of income. This is about Plan B too - Having multiple sources of incomes.

MEGHAVI VYAS

Meghavi Vyas is an internationally certified Image Management Consultant (USA) and Soft Skill Trainer (SQA-Scotland). She is a Civil Engineer who has moved from engineering buildings to engineering personalities for a decade now. She believes Image is one of the underutilized resources we have at our disposal for success in our life. Her brand promise claims, "Change your Image - Change your Life."

AN EMPLOYABLE IMAGE

In my initial days as an Image Management Consultant I had an acquaintance that was into placements. His job was to get jobs for people. One fine day we were having our routine conversation and in the middle of it he received a call. With a smile on his face and a sparkle in his eyes he picks up the call. In sometime the smile withered and the eyes lost the sparkle. By the time he finished the call his face was all gloomy.

Out of concern (also curiosity) I asked him the reason. To my shock I learnt that he had a candidate who went for an interview for the position of manager. He was absolutely confident of his credentials for getting the job.

However, he was almost slammed on the phone for sending a candidate who came in sandals for an interview.

There was no way he could get appointed, but I earned an opportunity to tie up and train his candidates going for interviews. This was one of my major work assignments.

This might get you thinking that do people really get a job just because they are well dressed, well groomed, better mannerisms; all in all, a positive image.

Of course not, and this I say as an Image Management Consultant. People get jobs based on their credentials; however, what we miss is that our image is also one of the credentials we have.

Let's understand this. The first step to the job is sending a resume/CV. How do we do that? Most often it is in a mail. Probably in post if it has to necessarily go as a hard copy.

Do we ever personally go to hand it over? I am sure nobody does.

So, my question to you is why can't the company have a look at your resume and hire you. Why do they need an interview? Your resume is loaded with all the details and credentials.

Yet, they want to meet you in person before the final call. WHY?

This is where your Image, your presentation, the softer side of you comes into picture.

Harvard research claims that during the interview, 85% of the time, your softer side is observed. They already know your eligibility. An interview is not to check your intelligence quotient; it is to observe your present-ability quotient.

This is the time those experienced eyes of an interviewer are trying to pierce through you and figure out what is the substance other than the degrees that you bring to the table.

How confident are you, how comfortable are you, how meticulous are you, how emphatic you are? Do they have a questionnaire for the same, NO, they observe.

So, what do they observe?

They observe your conduct. Your body language, your mannerism, your behavior, your level of comfort, way you dress, details of your grooming.

This entire package put together is the hyped term, IMAGE. And, I am sure you would now understand and agree to the importance of your image during an interview.

We all, invariably do these three second businesses called making first impressions. We meet people and in a snap of three seconds we make impressions about each other.

Do I need to remind you here, that first impression is the last impression? I am sure you know that.

Let us understand what works and what does not when you appear for an interview.

One basic thing as a pivot is to consider that what they think of you is your responsibility and not theirs. People judge you only based on how you present yourself – your dressing, grooming, body-language, mannerism is doing the talking while people make judgments about you.

You don't have any control over their judgement, but the good news is how you present yourself is totally-completely in your hands, only in your hands. Let us understand some standard.

Let us divide this in major four segments:
1) Dressing, 2) Grooming, 3) Body-language, 4) Mannerism

DRESSING

This is one of your most powerful resources. Use it to maxim. Least you can do is wear a neat, freshly pressed set of clothes.

Take care of three F: a) Function b) Fit c) Fiber

Function – Think of where are you going, who all would be there, what all tasks would you be involved with? This decides the most important factor of dressing – the function. For an interview scenario you want to dress in a manner that you are comfortable yet look formal. Opt for solid shirts in dull muted colors like blue, beige, ivory, off white, khaki, white etc. Avoid too light and too dark colors in shirts. It is advisable to wear full sleeves, but if you are going to fold your sleeves, half sleeves is a better choice. For the interview purpose it will be good to wear a light shirt and dark trouser.

Fit – You definitely do not want to appear wearing somebody else's clothes. Check for the fit at armpit, shoulders, chest, wrist (if it is full sleeves), the first button in case you need to wear a tie. Too loose or too tight is a distraction.

Fiber – In India where we have practically summer for almost ten out of twelve months, it is imperative to consider the fiber. Cotton is the best option you can have. Linen is a smart choice;however, you need to consider your commute since it gets crumpled fast. We also have a mix of cotton with other fiber which allows you to breathe but resists the wrinkle. Try out what suits the best for your needs and your budget.

GROOMING

This takes your first impression to the next level. A polished look is what you get from well-done grooming. For a typical interview scenario, no flying hair please. Make sure to have them under control. Tie them, use a gel whatever you may prefer to do.

For gentlemen, it's either a clean shave or a well-done beard. There is no in-between. For women, no facial hair and minimal makeup to give a neat look. A basic BB/CC cream with a lip gloss or nude lipstick with some kajal and mascara should be good enough for an interview. Neat nails and teeth go without saying. If your interview is post lunch, resist the temptation of having raw onion. A pair of polished shoes can help your career fly. A structured office bag is always better than a backpack.

BODY LANGUAGE

Your body talks more people take that more seriously than your words. Make sure you are aware of what you are communicating this way. Have a straight posture. Straight back, straight knees, stomach in and chest out; have this in your mind. While entering the cabin for an interview, be polite but not meek. Do ask for permission but don't lean unnecessarily.

Take care not to touch your face every now and then. Keep your hands visible on the table if you can.

MANNERISM

Between a course to handle your silverware or a master graduation, choose the former. The way you conduct yourself goes beyond the degree. The way you conduct yourself and the way you treat others goes a long way. Be on time – I mean ten minutes before your scheduled time. Be courteous with the staff. Don't litter your stuff in the waiting area. In case you pick up a magazine/newspaper make sure to fold it neatly and put it back. Do not try to add background music with your tapping feet. If you use the loo, make sure to flush and wash your hands. Smiling is the least yet most powerful thing you can do.

All the best for your next interview.
Go carry your smile with your certificates.

ANANYA NORI

Ananya is a Tsunami Survivor and corporate thought leader with almost two decades of experience in Banking, Telecommunications, Healthcare, HR, and Project Management. She is on a mission to empower corporate professionals to use techniques she learnt from Neuro Linguistic Programming (NLP) to apply in their day-to-day life to transform their career and achieve success in their lives.

PASSION SPEAK

When we work for any organization, we think we need to focus only on the job at hand. We assume single-minded focus alone would give us benefits in the growth, which is so wrong! Though many companies look for other volunteering opportunities, however many organizations still encourage the employees who are focused only on the current job, which should change.

There is a coinciding story of a man named Amit Paley and how he not only became the CEO of a Non-Profit Organization but also excelled in his job at McKinsey, according to Harvard business review.

Amit used to work as a journalist in the Washington Post for several years. He put long hours of work and did various stints in the war zone in the Middle East. Alongside he would serve on the board of his Alma Mater's Newspaper, where he got an opportunity to help aspiring journalists and learn how non-profit organizations work.

After leaving the job at Washington Post, Amit attended a B-School; from there, he went on to join as a consultant at McKinsey. He did not stop just by working single-mindedly at McKinsey, but he also ensured that he continued to volunteer.

Then he volunteered at the Trevor Project over weekend calls for LGBTQ (Lesbian Gay Bisexual Transgender and Queer) to prevent suicides among the youth. He eventually had an opportunity to join its board that gave him exposure to the operational and financial challenges of such groups and inspired him to get more involved in the Trevor Project. With all the experiences, involvement, and learnings, the results he produced eventually were terrific. Thereby, he went on to become the CEO of the Trevor Project in 2017.

By investing his time outside work, in things he was passionate about, he learned something that made him better at work at McKinsey. Amit Paley stated, "The experiences at The Trevor Project also prepared me for the future leadership roles that I would not have known. That's the power of strategically taking on extra tasks outside of your organization."

Coming back to my story, I lost interest in my job. I realized I worked hard in my company, only to get to the next level, after that another level; however, this cannot lead me to become the CEO of the company.

Then, I wanted to do something that excites me, to find that out I needed to explore. I made MLM sales at Amway, Tupperware, and Oriflame, yet I did not get any satisfaction.

Then, I got an opportunity to volunteer, within my limits, in my Company's Outreach Program. I could not visit in person due to the night shifts, and I had a son who was still young, etc. But then these small acts of kindness truly gave me something very precious – Compassion.

I became compassionate about the people and that I wanted to do something in return for the community, I wanted to serve people from the lessons, experiences, and knowledge I acquired. I understood that I should be able to speak up. I didn't exactly know what I could do. I learned that my time is minimal, and I needed to start using it wisely from now on.

Sometimes I wanted to reach out to people and help them, and at other times I would be sceptical if I could fulfil those responsibilities, I had self-talks, "What would others think of me?" which further confused me. The more I started to listen to what my intuition said; the desire to reach out became very strong. Then I noticed things slowly started to unfold one by one.

I became a founding member of the Professional Speakers Association of India (PSAI). There, I met a lot of awesome people, and one of those I met was Jogesh Jain (JJ), at the first-ever summit of PSAI in 2019. He found out that I had the desire to contribute and needed ways and means to spread my message.

Jogesh was very kind enough to offer me his program to get mentored. I was a part of his online coaching program from JJ School of Employability. I truly felt as if it was a strange blessing that showered through JJ. He trusted me. JJ is a very kind-hearted and down to earth person. He taught me various ways to extend my hand and reach out to everyone I could help.

Later, I joined Toastmasters Club so that I could learn the art Public Speaking. Things changed, and I had to drop the idea of toastmasters, due to the unavoidable circumstances in my family. However, I remembered JJ tell me, "When we speak from the bottom of our heart, we do not need to practice our speeches, and the words would flow effortlessly." JJ's words were convincing enough. I also realized, the discourses I frequently hear from Sadhguru, Mahatria, Dhandapani, Swami Paripoornanda, Suki Sivam, and few others, all of them speak from their acquired knowledge and not from any prepared speeches.

I also had to resign from my job and look after my kids, yet I was not worried about my newly acquired "Homemaker status." Since I had foreseen tremendous opportunities that JJ taught me. I got clarity to become a coach and completed the NLP Practitioner Course. If we look out of alternatives, we are sure to get what we indeed search. I gained clarity and decided to start my own coaching business, thanks to JJ.

AKSHAY REGHU

Akshay K Reghu is a business development professional who has immense love for food and passion for cooking. Being an award winner and having sufficient experience in the F&B industry, he is on a mission to motivate others with his own experience of tasting success with chaotic beginnings.

A FAILURE YESTERDAY BUT A WINNER TODAY

I was born in a family of four in Kerala. Growing up, I was never the brightest student unlike my brother, but I was always considered a child with a big heart and a big tummy.

While my brother conquered various goals such as being the class topper, a rising musician with a band of his own and being vice-captain of the cultural department, I was always known as the brother of a rising star;

I cared less. I always felt that nothing that I was taught or made to forcefully learn, interested me in any manner and because of that I was pathetic in subjects or in other words a failure to many.

The only thing that I loved was food and expressing my love towards the cooking art.

My mum always "shooed" that idea because having a hobby as a profession was a taboo during that time but instead wanted me to become a doctor as I apparently was "good at craft".

Definitely a sign which was misread by her. When I got my board results in 10th or the time to choose my path, even God didn't want me to become a doctor as he had other plans for me.

As you grow older, the "peer-pressure" of life starts to hit you. During my second year of graduation, my dad hit a rough patch in his business and that was the beginning of my life from worse to be an award winner.

After managing to complete my graduation with an above average score, I had taken up my first job in an American mortgage firm in Bangalore. My job was to make payments and data entry related work.

Being my first job, I got scrutinized for being the slowest in the team and was taunted even when I managed to give a 100% on quality, till one day, I lost it. This infuriated my reporting leader because now I was neither fast at my work nor having 100% in quality. Though he is a good human in life, his taunts made me question my capabilities in life.

While I used to pacify my parents that I was doing well at work, in reality I felt defeated and searched for comfort learning the art of cooking and binging on food. I went with the flow for a long time till I had to pursue my master degree.

Every Parent wants their kid to do the best in life and so did mine. My mother being the parent with high ambitions wanted me to take finance but again God had other plans and I was given an opportunity to learn marketing from a prestigious school in Bangalore which quite honestly fascinated me for once.

An important aspect of doing a Masters' degree is your domain internship but, in my case, there was a small mix-up. While I sat for the interview, I was told that there wasn't any internship role for marketing but a finance internship was available and asked if I wanted to give it a shot.

I thought why not? The interview would be a good learning experience even if I don't get the internship opportunity. I was asked the most basic questions to which I answered to my best but to my horror (and surprise), I was selected.

While I tried discussing this with my B-school, I was told that I won't be able to get another internship because of institutional policies. I gave the internship a shot but again I felt lost and failed miserably which resulted in binging on food and getting bigger in size.

Later after a month, my B-school understood the situation and gave me another internship in my domain. This was a well-known event organizing firm in Bangalore.

I was finally relieved that my life was starting to turn around but to my horror again my reporting manager was brutal when it came to work.

Though I enjoyed my work, my selling capabilities were bad and I was told that I would be a bad salesman. During this period, I had gained an immense amount of weight but for a change I was done being sorry for myself.

I decided to start hitting immediate goals to get my confidence back. They say for a healthy mind you need a healthy body and that's what I started with.

I reduced my weight drastically from 96 to 80 on my own and I hit my first goal to be on the right path.

Moving on, I completed my internship along with my Masters and I was placed in a reputed FMCG company as a B2B salesperson. I was assigned under the company's region head Mr. Guru, whom I was about to meet.

My life in the corporate world till that moment had been a bumpy directionless ride and I was wondering what God had for me now. With sweaty palms and a thumping heart, I opened the office door to be greeted by one of the humblest faces today.

Though I had a few stints in the corporate world, Mr. Guru treated me like a complete fresher and gave direction on how to proceed. Though my performance was initially what I felt was bad, he motivated me saying that I was doing good and always had my back.

He gave me direction on how to sell. This boosted my morale and I finally landed my first deal. I was proud beyond words; I achieved another goal. As time flew, I enjoyed what I did & I closed major deals solidifying my position in the market.

In a period of one year, during our annual meet, I was called on stage and was awarded a trophy for performance. I couldn't believe it; my entire journey till that moment had rushed through in my head and with a heavy heart, I whispered, I've done it!

Today not only am I a business development professional who guides individuals in sales but also to those trying to have a physical transformation with good workouts and healthy diets.

"Everyone has a path in life & at times it never comes easy, but with a change in mentality and effort, you will find your way, so never be disheartened."

MOHAMMAD ZEESHAN ALI

Zeeshan is a Learning Design Consultant and a passionate Digital Learning Expert. With 8 years of experience in the Learning Industry he wishes to disrupt this industry and take it to all the nooks and corners of our country. This will solve the unemployment issue of India to a great extent.

THE 'NEW' WAY OF LEARNING – E-LEARNING

With the onset of COVID-19 Coronavirus, the job market trends, approach, and requirements have changed completely. It will be extremely difficult for few industries such as Retail, Travel, Hospitality, Automotive, Oil & Gas, Real Estate etc. to overcome the crisis and make their business profitable. This means instability in the job market of such industries. This also means that our skill sets require a big overhaul and we need to unlearn many old methods and learn the most relevant ones.

Now, there are industries which show great potential to succeed in the current pandemic situation and promise a sustainable future ahead. These industries are Healthcare, Gaming, Insurance, Data Science, Spiritual Science etc. Among such industries, one which really stands out is the Learning **Industry** and specifically **Digital Industry**. As per Forbes research, e-Learning will be a USD325 Billion industry by 2025.

There are many organizations with their own Learning & Development (L&D) business unit which takes care of the learning needs of their respective organization. There are also service based organizations which act as an external vendor to serve the learning requirement of these companies. This is due to huge demand in the parent organization and shortage of manpower and skills in their respective L&D business unit.

The major learning needs through organizational learning initiatives are –1.

Product/platform Training	Software, Applications or Systems Training
HR, Regulatory and Compliance Training	Sales and Service Training
Workplace Safety	Quality and Processes
New Hire Onboarding	Soft Skill and Leadership

The above learning needs can be delivered mostly using learning product types such as Web Based Training (Level 1, 2, and 3), Instructor Led Training (ILTs), Virtual Instructor Led Trainings (VILT), Talking Head Videos (THV) or Motion Graphics Videos (MGVs), Quick Reference Guides (QRG), Job Aides (JA), Augmented Reality (AR) or Virtual Reality (VR), Gamification and many more.

In order to serve the training requirements using the various learning product types, the organizations from various industries require various skills and roles. The most in-demand skills and roles in learning industry are:

· **Instructional Designers:** They are the Learning Design Consultants who understand the learning needs of the customer and provide the best solution within the customer's budget. They have good communication skills (Verbal as well as written) and serve as a client facing role.

· **Graphics Designers and Video Motion Artists:** They are part of the media team and help Instructional Designers to bring the visualization and solution into reality.

· **Content Curators and Learning Management System (LMS) Experts:** They also play a very important role and maintain the content created by Instructional Designers and media teams on the LMS. The LMS helps the organization to perform all the functional requirements such as tracking, reporting, grading, online collaboration etc. to manage the learners.

All the three roles have a separate career path within the organization.

It is also important to have expertise on a few tools (not all) from the list of various eLearning authoring, graphics, and video editing tools. Further, you can build your expertise in other tools on the job depending upon your interest and expertise. Some of the important tools are:

A. **eLearning Authoring Tools (SCORM Compliant):** Articulate Storyline, Adobe Captivate, Lectora etc.

B. **Graphics and Video Editing Tools:** Adobe After effects, Adobe Premier, Adobe InDesign, Camtasia etc.

C. **Digital Adoption Tool:** WalkMe

These are the most in-demand roles and skills in the big corporate houses within the learning industry. They don't even think twice to meet your salary expectation if you meet their requirement. The demand is ever growing as the "New Ways of Working" has made it so. It is also important to note that the learning industry skill sets will help us in our day to day life and help us to build our personal digital brand as well.

In my opinion, the learning industry will be helpful in fulfilling **JJ School of Employability's vision** of reaching **709 districts** and impacting **10 million** people. If we align our students, fresher's, or one who need career transitions towards acquiring skill sets from the learning industry, it will create a huge impact in the society due to the huge demand in the industry.

In my opinion, the COVID-19 coronavirus global pandemic is a blessing in disguise for all of us, especially the new generation job seekers, students, and one who need career transition. But the burning question is still unanswered. The change is approaching. Are you ready?

Personal Experience:

I started my corporate career in the learning industry back in 2012. I am extremely fortunate for being a part of this industry as it has given me multi-fold growth and it is just a beginning. With more demand and lack of good Learning Design Consultants (Instructional Designers) in the market, you will always have edge over the management as well as job recruiters. The huge demand can be accessed from the fact that my 4-year-old CV still gets me job interview calls during the current global crisis. I have also noticed that my peers have switched their jobs during the COVID-19 Coronavirus crisis where there is huge uncertainty looming over the job market.

SUDARSHAN GOPAL

Sudarshan Gopal is a leader and a strategic thinker in technology and people management. He has a pragmatic approach to problem solving, has the ability to think laterally and to suggest creative solutions to complex business issues. With a broad experience in multicultural project management, he has the expertise in successfully adapting business concerns locally.

He also lends the expertise to companies willing to capitalize on insights in Quality Management, Systems and Processes. Has the ability to attract and retain technical staff, even during challenging conditions. He is a product expert with significant customer facing experience. Proven expertise in managing large scale teams across geographies and conflict Management.

THE RISE OF E-LEARNING

With COVID 19 emerging as the global health emergency, this is an unprecedented situation and adaptation and workplace evolution is going to be key across all companies with employment expected to see a brand new normal.

Emphasis will be on job security from professionals with their financial commitments and reluctance may be there to explore new opportunities.

However, industries such as healthcare and life sciences which are less impacted by pandemic, there could be some appetite to move jobs in this sector and also job types such as digital analytics and data science will be more open to switching roles in the technical industry.

This will trigger a change in the mindset of professionals and we can foresee a big wave of them wanting to change their lives and jobs.

With the Work from Home (WFH) option getting productive and being connected, professionals want this flexibility much more than before as they don't have to sit in traffic and the cumbersome commute time is removed. Thus, the shift towards virtual working space will be accelerated.

This will also create a demand for e-learning with dependency on the digital tools and increases the working efficiency by creating new opportunities for roles in engagement management. However, connectivity, remote team interaction and company culture will be a challenge for the employers.

JOB CHANGE/SEEKING

For professionals wanting to move jobs during this pandemic, assess first if there is an option of internal mobility to build your career within the company as making a shift in industries will be a bit of a challenge right now.

If not worried about immediate survival in the current lockdown, here's how the lockdown can be utilized for a positive impact on our career.

IMMEDIATE ACTIONS

Follow a proactive routine to manage time optimally and get the results you seek by working diligently with the daily team call routine. Volunteer for additional tasks online and deliver within deadlines so that new stuff can be learnt.

MEDIUM TERM

If the lockdown gets extended further, assess impact & make plans for the next 6 months of your services, mapping your industry with research on competition, suppliers, customers which will be critical for your job and your firm.

MACRO VIEW

Identifying our old way of being and thinking which is restricting our growth and how new learnings and thought processes can be implemented into our lives.

Contemplating on the meaning of work for us so that work is not sought for money and career becoming the source of our identity, independence and maturity, engagement and fulfilling an inner desire to contribute and make a difference so that future career satisfies our other latent needs apart from providing an income.

COMPLEMENTARY LIFE SKILLS DURING THE PANDEMIC

1. Elder Anchors - Rebuilding communication with elders and seeking their inputs to gain wisdom from their experiences.

2. Children Connect - Spending time to play their games increases trust, accelerates their learning, improves our parenting skills and opens vital communication lines for the future.

3. Surviving with Friends – Remembering our school buddies to connect with them and recreating good times to create resilience and optimism.

4. Staying Sane - By seeking sunlight through a walk in our building premises or a cup of tea on the balcony. Housework, physical exercise or short walks inside the house keeps us sane and refreshed.

5. Unrelated Skills - Nurturing our hobbies like reading, drawing, cooking, playing music etc. Developing these skills engages our mind to be sharp and get ready for a return to the professional world.

EMBRACING THE CAREGIVER

"Amma, I am going to the Mall along with my wife and son. Please take care of the house".

"OK Son. You go ahead. My legs are sore. I am not interested in coming to the Mall. You go ahead."

"Grandma, you should also come" insisted the grandson …

"Grandma cannot climb all those steps in the Mall. She does not know how to use the escalator. As there are no temples there, Grandma would not be interested. She is interested only in going to temples" said the daughter in law.

Though Grandma agreed with this statement, Grandson was adamant. He refused to go to the Mall if Grandma was not accompanying.Though Grandma repeated that she was not interested, she could not enforce her will against her dear eleven-year-old Grandson. She agreed to accompany them.

Grandson was very happy. Father asked everyone to get dressed up. Before her parents could get ready, the oldest and the youngest were ready. The youngster took his Grandma to the front room. He drew two parallel lines, a foot apart. He told his grandmother that it was a game and the old lady had to pretend that she was a Crane (Bird).

She had to keep one leg within the lines and raise the other leg by three inches.

"What is this my dear?" asked Grandma.

"This is the crane game Grandma. I will show you how to play." Both of them played a few times before the father could bring the Car....Grandma became adept in the game.

They reached the Mall and when they reached the moving steps (escalator), father and mother were wondering how the elderly lady would travel in that. Grandson took Grandma near the escalator and asked her to play the crane game. Grandma raised her right foot and kept it on one of the moving steps and raised her left leg by three inches and could easily reach the next moving step. This way, effortlessly she used the escalator to reach the higher level, to the wonder of her son and daughter in law. With her successful debut, Grandma and the grandson moved up and down several times on the escalator and were enjoying the fun.

They then went to the theatre to see a movie. As it was cold inside, grandson took out a shawl from his bag and covered the old lady, with a mischievous smile. He came prepared for this! After the movie, they went to the restaurant. When his son asked his mother for the dish to be ordered, his son took away the menu and thrust it in the hands of Grandma.

"You know how to read; better go through the menu and order whatever you want". Grandma decided about what she wanted to eat.

After meals, Grandma and the grandson played some video games. Before leaving for home, Grandma went to the toilet. Using that occasion, the father asked his son how he knew so much about his mother which as a son, he was not aware of.

Prompt came the response:" Dad, when a young child is brought out of home, how many preparations are made - milk bottles, diapers, wipes etc.!?.... Your mother would have also done all these things for you. Why not show the same consideration for your mother? Why did you presume that the elderly would be interested only in temples? They also have normal desires like going to the mall, enjoying all the fun. Since they may not openly express it, we have to compel them to enjoy these things".

Father was speechless. However he was happy that he learnt a new lesson from his eleven year old son.

Father was me, daughter in law was my wife and the kid was my son.

ZARINE SWAMY

***Zarine Swamy** is a writer, speaker and Career Coach. Her 16 years of Finance Leadership experience along with a passion for helping others and enabling change of the right kind empower her to be a mentor to corporates and individuals alike. She is on a mission - MISSION TRANSFORM WITH 'FAIRPLAY'. She is actively looking to remodel the dynamics of Success as we know it today through her book and her mentoring venture Success Valley. That is precisely why she has developed the FAIRPLAY model, which has actionable insights into the triplets of Success- the mindset or mental fitness, soft skills and hard skills. With hacks to change belief systems & build resilience, honest advice on individual brand building and networking the FAIRPLAY model is a success blueprint.*

F.A.I.R.P.L.A.Y

I have always considered myself to be talented. I was also professionally qualified from one of the best MBA schools and I have worked in some top corporates in India.

I am not blowing my trumpet; I am telling you my story,about what happened to me over the past couple of years. Despite having some very obvious things working in my favor, I was depressed and dejected. I could not fathom the path in which my career was headed. I began to doubt my abilities. It happens, and it happens to the best of us. Organizational gas lighting, politicking and control dramas are all fairly common.

What I needed was to actively seek and find my 'WHY'. In the process of seeking and finding, I found my purpose. I realized most of what had happened to me and was probably happening with very many hapless employees was the outcome of working for a bad leadership.

My mission is to transform the employability space with my venture 'Success Valley' by building future leaders who stand on integrity & put people first. This includes helping employees who have had their self-confidence eroded by bad leadership and organization culture regain their 'WHY', the way I found mine.

If you are the average salaried individual you spend more than 70% of your waking hours at work, if you are the average salaried individual, you spend most of that time pushing yourself unwillingly to show up at work and then run an obstacle race through workplace politicking for the rest of the day, this is not and should not be acceptable. You are unique and have one chance to live your best life, no matter where you are at present.

I have devised the 'FAIRPLAY' framework, a model for success I use in my coaching instructions- to enable just that. With unique insights into the triplets of mental fitness (mindset skills), soft skills and hard skills, the model debunks several popularly held perceptions of success.

The 'FAIRPLAY' model reveals that success- the long lasting, happiness inducing kind- comes from Integrity, Gratitude, Fairplay and basic Honesty. Apart from bringing 'goodness' back in fashion, it really works to transform your belief system and personality so you can develop a success blueprint.

The **'FAIRPLAY'** model in a gist

F

Your 'Faith' shapes you.

Every battle is won before it's ever fought. The secret to winning the battle in the mind is the difference between success and failure. As our beliefs/ thoughts->feelings->actions->results.

The key to success is in our belief system (our faith). There are no right or wrong beliefs, there are only supportive or unsupportive beliefs. It is important to choose supportive beliefs, to win the battle in the mind first!

A

'Abundance' is all you have.

Having an abundance mindset plays a huge role in the game of success. Abundance is believing that the Universe holds enough space and resources for all and we need to only have the right mindset to access these resources.

One can develop and use this weapon to their benefit through: Gratitude Support and Collaboration,aiming high i.e. taking moonshots. Having positive money beliefs, i.e. viewing money as a resource that can do great good. Speaking the language of choice.

I

'Involved' in the present.

The way to tap into supportive beliefs and abundant resources is for us to keep our mind rooted in the present. This is called mindfulness. It involves being 100% committed in the present moment and what we do in the present moment. A facet of a person who lives in mindfulness is accountability. Mindfulness also means holding our Integrity in the present moment, i.e. holding onto values, not selling out in the hope of a better future and keeping promises. When we live mindfully, our mind becomes more attuned to accept challenges. We face them head on to come out as winners.

R

'Resilience' is tough to fight

Resilience, or the ability to get up and move on, no matter what blows we are dealt with, is the one trait that separates the leaders from others. Resilience can be defined as the ability to go past illusions and view the correct reality. As beliefs->feelings->actions->results Resilience involves shaping the inner world to face challenges faced by the outer world.

P
Projecting the 'Persona'

The way we come across to ourselves is the way we come across to the rest of the world. When we love and accept ourselves, we become less needy. If our belief patterns about ourselves are supportive, we like ourselves and the world likes us back. The image we wish to convey to the world is as important as the image we have of ourselves. Of crucial importance is branding. Successful people build themselves up to create brand value.

L
'Leveraging' who you know

Networking to identify a mentor, whether we are on a salaried job or a business is important. A mentor's time can be valuably used to learn from, learn by observing and asking them for feedback. As the mentor – mentee relationship grows the mentor can sometimes turn into a sponsor. Networking to build relationships is equally important. The quid pro quo model can be effectively used in networking.

A
'Articulation' is never undervalued

Language can be used to work for us. Good corporate communication involves being assertive- but coming from a place of understanding and compassion. The art of negotiation is an important aspect of being articulate.

Y
The 'Yearn' for knowledge

We live in a VUCA world. Skill based learning is a must for survival and growth in this world. Learning can be academic- enrolling for courses and getting certifications. While this kind of learning is an asset to have especially in organizations which value credentials from reputed institutions, job based learning is essential. Job based learning is a continuous process. In the career path that we chart out a plan is needed for developing skill sets, and these need to be aligned to career goals.

DR. DHARMESH RAVAL

Dharmesh Raval is a management educator, researcher and all passionate about collaboration between academia and industry. With a rich experience of over 2 decades he understands ideal chemistry between academia and industry, and is exploring newer ways for helping both in creating value.

INDUSTRY ACADEMIA COLLABORATION

Collaboration has been a tested policy for many years and has helped individuals, businesses, industry and economies. Collaboration is a strategy to fight the situation and problems on hand and it presents an excellent opportunity to exploit the best among all the partners.

It is always an exciting idea to collaborate, when we people meet each other exchanging ideas and information. There are numerous instances when companies, individuals, government, experts, etc. interact with each other and it seems there are a lot of things which can be done together, but in the majority of cases they fail to materialize. And that is the reason that collaboration has been an effective strategy but it has not yielded the results it is capable of delivering.

In current times when all the players are working hard to find a new path out of the uncertainty arising due to pandemic, the need for collaboration is much bigger than ever before.

There are challenges and hurdles for Industry as well as for Educational Institutions and there is a dire need to search for complementary connections between Industry and Educational Institutions.

Collaboration is the key to unlock the unknown power of complementariness. There are numerous instances of partnerships and collaborations which have helped solve severe problems in the past and thus the power of partnerships and collaborations is proven.

But the million-dollar question is to implement such partnerships and collaborative projects.

THIS QUESTION CAN BE SUBDIVIDED INTO 5 SUB QUESTIONS:

- Academia industry partnership is not a new concept, but why still it is not widespread?
- It is a known concept but why still it is seen as an optional one?
- There are several models...but why not a single - all acceptable one has not emerged?
- Do we really buy in the fact that we may collapse if we fail to collaborate?
- If we agree to the need...How do we collaborate?

Industry-academia partnership has always been under wide deliberations in many ways. A well evolved mutual area of interest nourishes the relationship between academic institutions and industry in a bigger intention between knowledgeable professors and professionals in industries.

Core Strengths of Academic Institutions

Expertise in Teaching

Broad experience in Research

Availability of Training Infrastructure

- **Physical**
- **Information Technology**

Expertise of faculty members in high end areas

Courseware and Couse-packs for variety of skills sets

Ability to offer short term and flexi-hours course.

Institutes have exceptional high-end applied courses which fascinates the industry. Industry looks for human resources with proper applied knowledge in the field. Industry needs to impart proper training for its newly recruited trainee. Involvement of students with the industry makes a proper hit to reduce the gap. Another part of interest for the industry is the knowledgeable faculties and scientists who are doing globally appreciated research.

INDUSTRY IS THE GROWTH ENGINE OF ECONOMY

Industry is the growth engine of the economy, provider of employment and generator of livelihood for all the participants. It includes organized and unorganized sectors and includes several sectors.

It includes manufacturing as well as the services sector and it decides the future of any country. Apart from financial resources another very important resource that Industry is in need is human resources. It needs people at all levels to perform different functions to run the business.

It is important to understand Educational Institutions and Industry and their roles, this will help us in understanding if they complement each other. If Educational Institutions are creating talent in the form of passed out students and helping industry to prepare their teams of high performing individuals there are a lot of things that industry can offer to Educational Institutions. The sound research base at Educational Institutions should certainly contribute to the innovation in Industry.

DO ACADEMIA AND INDUSTRY COMPLEMENT EACH OTHER?

- Majority of students pursuing technical higher education are still looking for employment.
- It is natural and logical to prepare students as per the requirements/need of Industry
- **What** industry is looking for should be the core theme of **What** institute should teach!
- Partnership is possible if above condition is satisfied.

THE CONCLUSION

It is important that there is a permanent platform for facilitating discussion and action which may take the form of Joint associations with a sharp focus on partnerships and partnering for selected areas. There is a dire need to spend time together to understand each other's functioning, challenges and strengths. This requires visionary leadership at Institution as well as at Industry, and more than that an ambition to identify a common good.

There is a great opportunity to offer Joint Programs including Educational (academic) Programs, Industrial Training Programs / Courses for industry, long time duration like 2 - 3 years and short time duration like few hours on weekends. Tailor made programs can also serve the purpose if offered by industry for students and faculty members(internship), by academia for working professionals /employees (technical and managerial).

There may be Research Collaborations wherein Industry can look to research as an investment for sustained profits and growth. Academic research should be initiated at the requirement request of industry. Research can enhance the ability of a company to adapt to changes and the readiness to absorb changes in technology. It can help build leadership positions in leveraging the new technology for offering higher value. Research can also help in creating more value, decreasing cost and improving quality.

Active and full-time involvement of company and academic institutes are key for improving employability.

KASHMIRA SANGOI

Kashmira Sangoi (founder at Mind Miracles), is a career strategist, holistic mind development trainer, an expert Dermatoglyphics consultant and a smart-parenting coach. With 99% of satisfied students and parents over 6 years, she is on a vision and mission to guide them on 'What', Why' & 'How' questions concerning behavioral traits, parent-child relationship, academics, extra-curricular activities and career goals thus empowering to lead a stress-free, happy and successful life.

DERMATOGLYPHICS
- THE LIFE CHANGING TOOL

In Eighties, during my school days, students were majorly judged by their academic IQ and marks, and I wonder even today after 30/40 years there is almost no change seen in that thought pattern. I was an average student. No matter how hard I worked, but maths & physics used to bounce above. I also had exam fear. Passing out year on year, was a big sigh of relief. Though I was a prize winning dancer, a good artisan and well in people connect, unfortunately these things were overlooked. Sadly, our education system ignores other intelligences and focuses majorly on academics.

In 11th grade one of our family friend, a PSI, asked me to take tuitions of his children. I explained that I was not good enough to be a teacher but he asked me to give it a try and so I started. Her daughter was in grade 6th and son in 4th. I used to explain their chapters by giving different examples unless they didn't understand properly. One thing was very clear that these kids should not face the difficulties which I went through. All went well and kids scored good marks compared to their past year performances. Uncle Bal Singh (PSI) told that his son, who was not interested in studies earlier, started enjoying it. It was so satisfactory to hear that my efforts went in the progressive way. From that time, I felt an urge to help children lead a stress-free education. Started teaching few more kids. But then I had to concentrate on my graduation and later got married.

For next 15 years I got busy with my married life and 2 kids. Though enjoying that life, somewhere one emptiness remained as I was not able to contribute for other kids and for society. Finally, when I felt that my kids are now not so dependent, I decided to again start living up for my dreams. In inclination to do something special for kids, I searched for various options. And fortunately soon I came across the amazing science of Dermatoglyphics also called as Brain Mapping. Though it was new launch in Indian market, it had ancient roots, mentioned in Samudrika Shastra, a part of Indian Vedic tradition.

First I decided to get Brain-Mapping evaluation done for me, to my hidden potentials and to know whether I was suited for this profession. Also there were plenty of players in this field pan India.

So was difficult to know whose system is accurate and authentic. Being a brain-mapping consultant was going to be a big responsibility on my shoulder for guiding a child, a parent, a student, a professional and helping them to reach a destination which they are meant for. So I went in deep search with each company. After interacting with 32 companies and getting 14 reports done for me, finally I found the authentic source.

In consultation over my report, I was astonished to hear the reason why I was average in studies and good in dance and arts. Had I known this in my childhood, I could have improved in my academics by working on relevant remedies. Anyways though not me, now I had this amazing tool that could help lots and lots of other kids, students, adults out there and also help fulfil my purpose of life. Dermatoglyphics and its application requires deep study. It isn't a mere 3-day franchise training. So then I invested plenty to get thoroughly trained from different sources which were national and international trainers and also read many books regarding the same.

I just fell in love with this amazing science as this gives precise solutions after analysing the root cause of every problem. It also helps to identify the core competencies, major limitations in academics, personal and professional life. In short it leads to a stress-free and happy life. And yes very important, all this goes 'Without asking a single question'. Yes, you heard me right. Our finger prints are blueprints of our brain.

All the 10 fingers have connection with different lobes of our brain. Left brain controls the right body and right brain controls the left part. Similarly, left hand's fingerprints matches with right brain and vice-versa. Our thumbs connect with Pre-frontal lobe (Action zone), Index connects with Frontal lobe (Think zone), middle finger connects with Parietal lobe (Kinesthetic zone), ring finger connects with Temporal lobe (Auditory zone) and little finger with Occipital lobe (Visual zone). If one is well equipped and trained enough to justify this beautiful science then I assure you, it will lead you to a happy and successful life, provided you get the evaluation done from an authentic consultant and work on the remedies suggested by him/her. Unfortunately, there are only 10-15% whom you can rely upon with this science. Other 85-90% practising it are knowingly or unknowingly risking people's lives because of their lack of proper knowledge and buying software from unauthentic fancy companies instead of hiring an authentic System.

Also these practitioners analyse the fingerprint types and ridge count with half knowledge and thus, the entire interpretation fails. Many feel that miscounting only one ridge may not make much difference, but in fact it actually miscounts in lakhs of neurons in that particular brain lobe.

About Dermatoglyphyics: It is a branch of human morphology that studies the skin relief of the palms and soles, where the skin is covered with patterns of numerous ridges (papillary lines). The ridges are linear thickenings both within and the surface of the epidermis. They begin to develop in the human foetus by the 3rd month, but they do not appear on the surface of the skin until the 18th week. The papillary lines and patterns do not change with age nor are they affected by surrounding conditions. They exhibit considerable individual variability; many of their particular features are transmitted by heredity.

The results of Dermatoglyphics are therefore used widely in criminology, forensics, medicine (in cases of disputed paternity) and clinical medicine (for early diagnosis of certain chromosomal diseases). Extensive study of skin patterns has revealed right-left, sexual and territorial differences, which are used in anthropology for example, to detect kinship between various human groups and to study the bilateral symmetry of the body. Skin patterns are also used in comparative anatomical studies of man and in anthropological genetics (familiar and twin studies).

References:

1. Gladkova, T.D.Kozhnye uzany kisti I stopy obez'ian I cheloveka. Moscow 1966.

2. Cummins, H. and C. Midlo. Finger Prints, Palms and Soles. New York, 1961.

3. The Great Soviet Encyclopaedia, 3rd edition (1972-79)

By getting one's dermatoglyphics evaluation done we come to the quantitative and qualitative traits of an individual. Every fingerprint has its own characteristics, behaviour traits. It represents how the person will take input, think, act or react, what would be the thinking pattern, would it be cognitive, reflective, affective or reverse.

Whenever brain receives an input all the lobes start to process, the one with highest quantity of neurons and fastest quality (type of fingerprint) will act first, our brain goes on an auto-pilot mode and react. Through this evaluation we come to understand the uniqueness we are born with, our personality, SWOT analysis, learning style means are you a Visual learner, Auditory or Kinesthetic learner through which learning becomes easy, board selection for a child, stream selection, extra-curricular activities, career suitability, partner compatibility, corporate placements, parenting, teacher's training and more. Like a manual received in your mobile box, it serves as a guidance for whole life journey.

I would like to share some success stories of my clients, that surely would amaze you

One of them was a student in the 2nd year of engineering having a back in the first year and failed in the second one. He was immensely disappointed and depressed. After the evaluation of his brain map I suggested him to choose career as historian or an archaeologist. The neural density in the brain lobe required for engineering was present in scarce amount. He admitted that he wanted to pursue archaeology but was forced by his parents to pursue engineering just coz his sister was a successful software engineer. I explained his parents to not compare their children. Fortunately, his sister was supportive and the boy had a sigh of relief when his parents understood that each child is unique and is more important than any degree.

Another boy who completed his 12th commerce was under pressure by parents to pursue BMS, which he wasn't intending for and wanted to be guided for some good career option. After evaluating his brain map, I suggested him to undertake IATA. He pursued it and got a good job in a reputed tours and travels company. He was really happy and said that taking decision to get the evaluation was the best decision! girl wanted to do MBA but wasn't sure in which stream and while we were explaining about this amazing science her father decided to get it done for him too. He was doing a job in the IT department at a good post and this sector requires high logic. But according to the evaluation his logic quantitative part was not good enough. So I asked him frankly, "Sir, you might not be loving your job, and might want to resign, is it so?".

That gentleman was shocked to hear this. He agreed and said that he always says this to his daughter.

I even suggested him that he has a potential to be a good cook and he agreed that he loved cooking too but due to family responsibilities didn't quit his job. One boy who was in International board came in 8th for stream selection. I suggested to go for Commerce, after 10th he came for Career guidance then I told him to opt for CA, this boy cleared all his CA related exams at 1st attempt. That doesn't mean that one should not work hard. This science shows you path but you have to walk on it.

I have many such examples. Even I wonder that how fabulous this tool is, when done by a reliable source and would make wonders in the employability sector. If the potentials and core competencies of an individual are channelized in the right direction, we can eliminate the 'trial and error' round and make the investments of time, money and efforts in the perfect path.

This science is not only for strugglers, as one of my mentors says "Catch them Young". And I am truly grateful to all my mentors and am even grateful to Jogesh for giving me this opportunity where I can share my insights on the industry I belong. Kids can easily work upon the remedies suggested for their overall development as our brain is under immense development in the early stages. They can focus on their strengths and overcome their weaknesses. They can also be guided on their hobbies which can be developed into a potential career.

It is possible to give specific career guidance based on Dermatoglyphics (neuro-scientific evaluation). Are you suited for sales, marketing, human resources, research, administration, operations, accounts, finance, architecture, designing, animation, humanities, fine arts, performing arts, psychology, sociology, law, engineering, medical, culinary arts or anything else? What are your preferences in colours, food, fragrances, hobbies, games? Are you a team player or a solo player? Are you a fast or slow driver? You name it, this science has it. This has answers for all your doubts without even asking a question. "Know innates, No doubts"

I truly believe, everyone is born for a purpose. If you unleash your potential, then you can easily convert your passion to your profession.

"Don't pick a job with great vacation time; pick a career that doesn't need escaping from. Choose a career where every working day is like vacation for you."

SURAJ KHOPKAR

Suraj Khopkar is an IT professional having 9+ years' experience in Telecom/Healthcare domain. With nearly a decade of experience in Software Testing, he is on a mission to explore Crowd Testing platforms and start the same.

MAKING A LIVING AS A CROWD TESTER

Freelance is a term which is barely heard in a country like India where people believe that work is being attached to a company and having a fixed time with a fixed salary!

For the past few months, the entire world is fighting a pandemic. This has affected business across the world badly and has a tremendous negative impact on the economy. We all know in current situations firms across various fields/sectors/technology are downsizing. On the positive note, this lockdown period presented an opportunity to upskill, learn new things and have a secondary income source.

I am working as a QA Professional for a reputed MNC in India. I have been working from home for the past 2 months. Apart from working, there was lots of free time as I hardly went out. It was on 26th April when I attended a webinar by Jogesh sir. It was enlightening for me. I asked myself this question – Am I utilizing my skill to full potential?

I signed up instantly and went through the crowd testing websites. These websites were paying people to find bugs/defects on dedicated websites and moreover you can work anytime! As I had time, I thought of taking this seriously and earning some money.

Crowd Tester is a term I found out for the person who is a freelance tester. As the software is being tested by people across the globe, we, the crowd and hence **Crowd Tester**.

Let's cut these things and get right through the process of becoming a Crowd Tester.

THERE ARE FEW RULES WE NEED TO TEACH OUR SELF:

- Have patience, a lot.
- You just keep testing! Money will follow. Better late than never.
- Know what to test first and what not to.
- Invest in mobile phones and upgrade it when required.
- Believe that you can earn, and You will!

THE PROBLEM WITH FREELANCE/UPWORK WEBSITES

In these websites, you need to bid for a testing project which are very less compared to development projects available. As you are a fresher on these websites, finding a project to test right away is exceedingly difficult.

HOW CROWD TESTING HOLDS UP AGAINST UPWORK WEBSITES?

In Crowd testing websites, you need to sign up and there would be no entry fees. Few websites take eligible candidates through a simple entrance test based on the basics of testing (to eliminate posers and recruit genuine testers as they pay well for eligible testers). There is no bidding! You can choose the website of your choice and start testing immediately. You can interact with other testers and learn the type of issues they log. You get paid a bonus if you have a specific device, they request for in the test cycle and for test case execution.

Here are the Crowd Testing websites I work with.

1. TestBirds
2. TestIO
3. UberTesters
4. CrowdSprint
5. uTest
6. MyCrowd
7. Testlio

TIPS AND TRICKS TO WIN IN CROWD TESTING WEBSITES

- iPhone apps are tested less as most people do not own them. Test those apps.
- Be the first to log an issue. Keep your Bug report template ready and copy paste the issues quickly.
- Purchase used mobile phones. It's good to buy stock android phones.
- Check out the issues logged by top testers. This will educate you on the type of issues that you were unable to find.

The earning is genuine. You will get paid. You need to spend some time in knowing how these websites function and then you can start playing around.
Happy Testing.

PRAVEEN SAH

Praveen Sah is a sales professional with over a decade of experience in the healthcare industry. A passionate individual driven by optimism and faith. An avid animal lover and a curious traveler who likes to turn experience and memories into the nutritious feed for mind, body and soul.

THE BLIND MAN WHO MADE ME SEE

It is said that the Eyes are one of the most beautiful gifts of God! Eyes are windows to the world. It's like a screen which plays our memories and most cherished life moments. We all observe and learn through eyes.

But what about people, who don't have this gift of seeing the world through eyes, I believe they have a larger role to play and that is inspiration and passion.

Learning and realization happens when you want it to happen. Passion needs courage, it keeps you going and growing throughout your life. The incident I am going to share with you, will surely make you go and will deliver what never say die attitude is!

This enlightenment happened to me in a Mumbai local in the year 2011. For those who live in Mumbai, travelled to or have spent few years in Mumbai must be knowing that Mumbai locals are not only the lifeline of Mumbai city but also a depiction of daily struggle which almost every one face as the sea of people is always wanting to make a way inside the local to grab a seat (if they are lucky !) or space to reach their destination. Can you imagine the challenge? or in fact it is the first hurdle which you have to cross to make yourself adapted to Mumbai life.

Now because we can see, we can plan which seat to rush to, look for the space to fit ourselves. I am a sales professional and to meet my clients, Mumbai local was my daily mode of commute. A lot of hawkers selling keychains, notepads, pens etc. used to enter the locals at one station and exit at some other station.

I remember the day, it was somewhere around 3pm and I was coming from a client meeting, somehow that day at that time, the rush in the local was bearable and surprisingly there was no passenger sitting in front of me.

So, for those who haven't travelled in a Mumbai local, it's like any other train with a layout of a metro train, when you enter you can either go and sit/stand to the right or to the left.

Sitting on the left side, confused and low on energy and passion somewhere lost in my own thoughts which were sucking energy and enthusiasm out of me, entered someone who forever changed my perspective about life. It was a Blind man who made me see!

With a smile on his face and confidence in his posture, the man was a hawker and was selling keychains, notepads, and pens to name a few. As soon as he boarded the local, he turned towards the left and started selling in his strong convincing sales pitch full of passion and energy.

But you know what? there was not a single person sitting on that part of the train. After delivering the sales pitch and telling about what he was selling in a unique manner with a smile, he paused for a few seconds just expecting someone would call and buy a pen/notebook from him but no one did.

This particular moment moved me into emotions and made my eyes moist. The man got down in the next station and disappeared in the sea of people. He left but his passion, courage, smile and hope stayed forever.

In my entire commute to my place, I was just thinking about how tough it would be for that guy every day to leave his home, struggle to navigate towards the local station, fear of tumbling on footpath, being extra cautious on not crashing with people around.

His passion and never say die attitude kept him going, overcoming every obstacle to reach his destination and do something full of contentment and satisfaction at the end of the day. He might not be able to sell big every day, but still I believe his effort to meet daily needs in such circumstances with dedication and passion was an eye opener for me.

On that day I learnt and saw what dedication, will power and self-respect looked like. I made a promise to myself that come what may, I will be the guy who is passionate, hopeful, strong and optimistic.

When I am writing this experience, I feel grateful and inspired to that *Blind man who made me SEE!*

SURESH TK

Suresh TK *is a national level basketball player and corporate thought leader. With 2 decades of experience in the IT Industry, he is currently a Senior Manager with Amadeus, a travel technology company.*

He is on a mission to empower corporate professionals to use the Sports Agility Mindset in their day-to-day life to transform their career and achieve greater success.

SPORTS VALUES FOR LEADERSHIP

Leaders are value-driven and their behavior and decisions are always based on underlying values. They never compromise on the values based on convenience or when faced with challenging situations. Every Leader should define values for themselves and lead by them.

I call this value system as FLAIR and every Leader should lead with FLAIR.

We can learn these values from Industry experts or some real-life examples from fields like sports.

A sport is not just a physical activity which ends in winning or losing. It teaches us several important values and life-lessons. I would like to introduce the Sports Agility Mindset, which is about applying sports values in the corporate life to achieve success.

Let us look at the FLAIR values and understand through sports examples and how Sports Agility Mindset can be applied

FAITH & COURAGE

A Leader must have faith in the organization's vision, mission and values. Conviction supported by data will always instill the courage to take decisions that are in the interest of the organization. Decisions will have to be taken that might not be popular, have risks associated and even may fail.

When things go wrong due to the decisions made by the team, the leader must stand by the team. It is important to explain the intent behind the decision taken when it has a larger impact.

We all remember the 2011 cricket world cup, when Indian team won the finals with Sri Lanka. MS Dhoni had faith in himself and went up the batting order when India was 3 wickets down. He displayed the courage to take it on himself as a Leader and lead by example.

SERVANT LEADERSHIP

Servant Leader is the one who is a servant to the mission or goal. The leader must instill this aspect in the team and make sure the team does not feel they work for the leader rather for the organization's vision and themselves.

A leader should be able to remove impediments in the team's work and ensure the team is productive and focused on project execution. The leader should aim to bring the best out of each team member and make them perform at their highest potential.

More importantly Leader should resolve the cultural differences and inculcate team bonding and team spirit. We all know about the top Indian shuttle badminton player, PV Sindhu. She recently won the world badminton championship and is amongst the top ranked players in the world.

The best badminton players come from Pullela Gopichand's academy and he is the one who has played a major role in the success of all these players. The way he nurtures the players and has contributed to the country by representing our players all over the world. A classic example of Servant Leadership.

AUTHENTICITY

A Leader needs to be authentic when it comes to addressing the team. There has to be transparency regarding information that matters to the team and address the concerns raised by the team to management with transparency. Team should be able to trust the Leader and be able to share their opinions and voice their concerns.

The Leader has to display consistency in behavior be it during good times or challenging times. Let us look at the example of Virat Kohli, One of the best cricket players and captain of Indian cricket team. The way he carries himself, his expression on the cricket field is an example of authenticity.

Be it with the opposition or his own team players he always speaks his mind and displays the same aggression and passion. He backs the team when the team has lost a match and challenges them equally to perform better. What you see is what you get.

INTEGRITY

A Leader should lead with example when it comes to Integrity. A Leader should know how to handle sensitive information like salary, performance rating, confidential data. A Leader should sensitize the team when it comes to critical information and build that maturity and culture within the team to instill the same seriousness of Integrity that he or she follows.

Examples of lack of integrity are taking personal printouts or submitting false claims, handling money or submitting travel expenses that were not incurred. Given the situation today due to COVID 19, Work From Home has become a norm and as a Leader we need to ensure the team is productive and responsible for delivering the tasks assigned to them.

My friend Sambhaji Kadam, joined Indian Army in 1998 and since then has played 17 years nationals for services team and 15 years for country. Post his playing career, he took up the role of Coach.

I remember an incident when he came to Bangalore as Assistant coach for the Senior Indian Men's team. It was the day when the dressing kit arrived and it was kept in the hotel room.

Sambhaji looked at the kit and the first thing he did was to pray and thank the almighty for the opportunity to represent the country as Assistant Coach. Sheer display of love for country and integrity.

RESILIENCE

Fail Fast, Learn Fast and Recover Fast should be the mantra of a resilient Leader. A resilient leader should never be afraid of experimenting and failing. This brings in the culture of innovation and trying something new.

Most of the work in the IT industry is monotonous and the experimentation aspect brings the change for the team to break the routine and help explore. When something goes wrong the leader should demonstrate solidarity and stand by the team and focus on the learnings rather than looking for the one who caused the issue.

During difficult times the team will always look up to the Leader for support and guidance. The Leader has to develop a resilience mindset to think innovatively during challenging times and help the team come out strongly.

Mangte Chungneijang Mary Kom is an Indian Olympic boxer and only woman to become World Amateur Boxing champion for a record six times. She was awarded the Padma Vibhushan, India's second highest civilian award, in 2020. She came from a poor family and her parents were farmers. When she was 15, she took the decision to leave her hometown to study at the Sports academy in the state capital Imphal. After her marriage she took a break from boxing, had 3 kids and later came back and in 2010 won the gold medal Asian Women's Boxing championship.

TANUSHREE NAIR

Tanushree Nair is an ex-IT professional turned social entrepreneur. She is an author of "Bring out that Red Lipstick" and currently working as an Energy Transformation & Mindset Coach. She is passionate about her mission to reach a million women reconnect with their feminine energies to lead a conscious, purposeful, powerful and successful life. She runs two unique energy & mindset changing programs called "The Soulful Living Program" & "REBOOT: Feminine Energy Mastery Program.

SYNERGIZE YOUR ENERGIES

The concept of energy is a vast and deep ocean. Our energies are interconnected and form a huge vibrational field. We all draw our energies from a universal cosmic source. Imagine a huge tank or limitless reservoir of energy and we are all drawing our life-enhancing energies from it! Energy also known as Prana, Chi, Qi in different civilizations is what connects our physical selves to the cosmos or the universe.

I have been particularly interested about this duality of energies within us- masculine and feminine. Regardless of gender, each of us has this expression of dual energies. As they call in tantric philosophy- Shiva (masculine) and Shakti (feminine) or Purusha (masculine) & Prakriti (female), these dual energies have their own qualities and characteristics. For ex: When we say that a boy is too sensitive and emotional where as a girl is a "tomboy", it just means that the dominant energies or what we call as their core energies is highly masculine or feminine.

Masculine Energies	Feminine Energies
Action	Flowing
Strength	Intuitive
Survival	Knowing
Security	Creative
Logic	Magnetic
Structure	Nurturing
Organizing	Emotional
Will Power	Empathy

Clarity	Receptive
Knowledge	Kindness
Linear	Dynamic

How do these core energies work and how do we unlock them to propel us in our life and work? You might want to ask - Is this topic a lesson in spirituality? No, it is not.

Then how does this tie-in to employability or us being employable? Good question!

The recent COVID-19 crisis has changed the definition of a lot of things and preconceived notions around us- the way we live, the way we meet, the way we communicate, the way we work, the way we look at our personal and professional lives. The manner in which a virus has derailed countries, economies, unsettled our lives and our jobs is nothing more than a grand lesson in the Universe's big scheme of teaching us "opportunities in adversity".

Back in 2000-01 was one such case. The Dotcom burst and the Twin Towers incident sent ripples in the entire employment and IT industry. The severe recession put people out of jobs, those who graduated (like me) were out of the market even before they entered it. All appointment letters, travel assignments cancelled and there were lay-offs/pink slips overnight. I remember me and my friend personally dropping 35 resumes as a fresher in blazing sun, in each of the offices in Andheri, SEEPZ (the first of the SEZ's in Mumbai, those days which housed all the big names in IT industry). I did not get a call from even a single one of them.

So, what does employability really mean?

Well, the dictionary says it is- "the quality of being suitable for a paid job".

What are those qualities which make us "employable"?

Is it the degrees/diplomas/certifications, accolades, achievements, experience?

To some degree, Yes.

But there is more to being employable than just on-paper achievements. The inner qualities of an individual play a major part on how an employer perceives us fit for a role, team and job. Problem- solving, collaboration, adaptability, organizing skills, resource management, creativity, networking, right attitude, drive, professionalism are some of the qualities apart from experience, that an employer looks in a candidate. We keep our resumes updated but how many of us have really focused on honing these personal strengths before applying for an employment opportunity?

I have been exploring the field of energy work for the past 15 years. It gave me a lot of insights as an individual and also in my career. During these years, I have realized how the interplay of masculine- feminine energies subtly affects us and how our activities and actions affect our energies.

The masculine energies have been great to build world-order, enforce laws, build empires, build processes, big corporates, run economies. In that bargain, we suppressed the expression of our creative and free-flowing feminine energies. The gentle touch of feminine energies of empathy towards self and others, nurturing our trusted circle (networking with compassion), dynamism is very much required in the container of structure and discipline of the masculine energies.

Both go hand- in-hand. The feminine energy quality of being adaptable and dynamic is so much more relevant today with such an unsettling and fast-changing world. How many of you have really thought about these intrinsic qualities as an addition to your resume?

We tie our success and failures to situations and challenges. Our self-worth is dependent on how high we have reached up the corporate ladder or what is my pay package. Have I bought a house in 5-10 years, have I got that promotion, have I got numerous prestigious awards and certifications?

How adaptable and resilient are you to wade through challenging situations like recession, slump, economic downfall, loss of jobs like we have been seeing every decade? There is no such thing as a work-life balance. We forget that work is a part of life and not a whole. We make work bigger than life and that's where the balance tips.

I cannot always control what goes on outside. But I can always control what goes on inside.
  -Wayne Dyer

My Inner Shakti framework addresses exactly this- Looking inwards and creating self-awareness., resilience, adaptability to mould oneself to handle any situation. Align yourself with your higher purpose. Make your foundation strong.

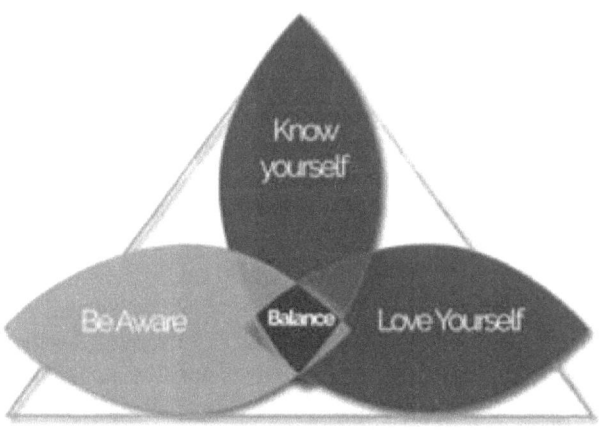

THE 3-PRONGED APPROACH OF THE INNER SHAKTI FRAMEWORK

- **Be Aware** – Aware of imbalances and that a change is required. Be in the here and now.
- **Know yourself** – Knowing your core energy and harnessing the strengths to balance yourself.
- **Love yourself** – Being kind and empathetic and loving yourself as you are.

Take charge and balance these energies to strengthen your being and express the strength of both your masculine and feminine energies. Upgrade yourself to have a conscious, fulfilling, purposeful, harmonious and joyous life.

Life is not about how fast you ran, how high you jumped, but how well you bounce
-Vivian Komori

RAJESH RAMAMURTHY

Rajesh Ramamurthy is an Aviation Professional with close to three decades of experience in Airline Operations, Consulting, Client Management & Training. Currently he is on an academic mission that will see him play a mentor to the next wave of Aviation Professionals.

MENTORING
– ARE YOU READY TO EXPERIENCE A NEW HIGH?

The mediocre leader tells. The good leader explains. The superior leader demonstrates. The great leader inspires." extolled Gary F. Patton.

Looking back at my career of 28 years in the Aviation Industry, this statement has never been truer in my case. This only makes me wonder whether it is high time to shift into what Gary Patton has expressed so beautifully as I try to answer the question *"Can You Be The Mentor You Never Had?"*

A year back during an extremely critical period of my life, I stared at oblivion, not knowing what I would do for a future. I had taken the bold decision to quit a high paying job because I felt I wanted to do something different. Now what was different, I never knew. I have always felt when you come from the state of the unknown, you are more open and receptive in terms of gathering information, analyzing it, and then using it to come to a useful conclusion.

During this state of the unknown, I came across Jogesh Jain, an unassuming person, who advertised himself as 'India's first Employability Coach" and was armed with the mission of helping people find their dream jobs. Sounded interesting to me and I immediately got onto the call to explore more. A few conversations later, I was enrolled into a program that was called "*New GEM (Generation Employability Mentor).* For the sake of brevity, I would call it as *N-GEM*

As the program commenced in the summer of April 2019, I got a deep revelation about what it means to have a mentor. In a world that is so digitally driven and places high expectation on the younger generation to become self-reliant, this experience took me to the era where students learnt the ropes through the experience of the teacher. This is where I feel mentoring is a powerful tool even in the midst of the digital disruptions. It would be interesting to understand how mentoring actually works and the framework, which I feel has no parallels So, what is mentoring and what frameworks work in my view.

The origin of the term mentoring dates back to the time of the ancient Greek storyteller, Homer. The modern usage of the term comes from the work of a French writer called Fenelon in the 18th Century.

KEY FRAMEWORKS

Look Inside- The Awareness Key

"Awareness precedes change." **says Robin Sharma.** As a mentor, it is particularly important to have this crucial conversation with your mentee. In my personal experience, becoming aware of your thoughts, aspirations are a key ingredient to your journey. Honestly speaking in the corporate world, we are quick on the update when we need to perform SWOT analysis for our teams, on new projects etc., though we may always hesitate to do so when it comes to our own selves.

As a mentee, the first step I took was to list down what my strengths were, what I actually wanted to do. Driving self-reflection is the first step. This can be achieved through documented questionnaires and what I love to call as "Crucial Conversations".

THE SECRET SAUCE- YOUR NICHE

The legend behind Walmart, Sam Walton, professes that "If everybody is doing it one way, there's a good chance you can find your niche by going exactly in the opposite direction.

The second step is looking for the secret sauce that makes the dish exciting and becomes the cynosure of all eyes at the table during the meal. This process is extremely important for a mentor to help the mentee, what is your niche. Believe me, as a mentee, this is not easy. There are very few people who can identify this at one go, while many struggle to choose from various options. It is where the role of the mentor is crucial.

Through a series of questionnaires, evaluations, the mentee can come to identify his/her niche or take a step in his/her "micro niche". It is ok to have multiple niche's, but what will drive your success is your micro niche. This becomes a corollary to the first framework of a deep assessment of your strengths. In my view, your strengths are the building blocks to the identification of your niche.

The Devil is in the detail, however trivial it is...

Imagine a scenario where you stitch a fabulous shirt with your tailor and find that the shirt has no buttons. Buttons are a vital aspect to any shirt without which the product is sheer waste. *The great fashion guru Christian Dior rightly said "The detail is as important as the essential is. When it is inadequate, it destroys the whole outfit".*

As a mentor, it is important to guide the mentee to make those fundamental changes. Our beliefs very often shape the way we respond to change. At the risk of generalizing, whether we are beginning our career or have made massive inroads into it, we often overlook the fundamentals.

A mentor is often like an organized calendar that keeps reminding you of your tasks at specified time. Even legends of the game like Sachin Tendulkar would always go back to the nets under the watchful eyes of their earliest mentors to iron out their flaws.

My experience in this program was that I had to focus on the smaller stuff. Networking Basics on platforms like LinkedIn, the need to work on the most basic aspects of your resume for more visibility were some of the trivial but most important insights that I learnt. It is important to sometimes overlook the oft quoted statement which says "Don't sweat the small stuff"

PREACH WHAT YOU HAVE PRACTICED

"Why do you not practice what you preach?" says St. Jerome.

As a mentor, it is important to not get carried away into a teaching mindset. The most beautiful part of mentoring in my view, is preaching what you have practiced. The mentor brings to the table a structure of the experience that he/she has personally undergone. A mentor does not show you how it is to be done, he/she only tells you how they have done it.

Can you clap with one hand- What a mentee needs to do in a mentor-mentee relationship?

- **Dump the baggage-** Let go of the excess baggage before you commit to the mentor
- **Whole Body and Mind involvement-** Ensure you are available both physically and mentally before you undertake your journey
- **Be vulnerable & open to learning-** It is ok to expose your weakness. Your weakness and your willingness to learn will open the doors to your strengths and ultimate success

As a N-GEM, I have realized that mentoring is indeed a powerful tool. A coach works on enhancing your potential, but how do you reach a state of achieving your basic potential before you enhance it, in my view here the egg always comes before the chicken

My mentor said, 'Let's go do it,' not 'You go do it.' How powerful when someone says, 'Let's!'" — Jim Rohn

PRABHAKAR BETHI

Prabhakar Bethi is a Marketing and Branding Coach, Mentor, Trainer, Author, and Launch Your Idea Online Specialist. My mission is to help 100,000 sales and marketing professionals to fast track their promotion to achieve greater success in their career and life.

EMPLOYABILITY
– THE ART AND SCIENCE OF IT!

Earlier it used to be like you acquire a degree in some field, professional or otherwise, like commerce, or get trained in some vocational course, you would get a job and gradually grow in your industry. At least it was like that when I entered the job market 30 years back.

With the time and technological advancements, the employment scenario has changed. With a greater number of people with professional qualifications getting into the job market but lacking the practical job skills, life skills and knowledge required to perform on the job, things have got complicated.

That's when Employability as a concept has received immense attention and gained huge importance.

I will condense and share my practical learnings from 25 years of corporate working plus 5 years of entrepreneurial and consultant and coaching experience. My advantage is that I have seen both the sides, very closely- one as an employee and second as an employer.

As I have come up from the bottom of the pyramid and reached the top level in the corporate, I have gained some very important insights into how as a professional you can turbocharge your employability so that your career graph will continue to zoom.

There are 3 things that are crucial in keeping your employability at peak level –
1. Your unique skills that are essential to your particular job
2. Your practical knowledge to deliver what is expected from you
3. Your attitude towards company, colleagues, superiors, situations, challenges you face in your job

The first two aspects, the job specific skills and industry related knowledge, to large extent are part of "Science of Employability" and will vary depending on your domain, it is the third aspect, the person's attitude, that is "Art of Employability" which will make a huge difference in how employable you are.

If skills and knowledge is hardware, the right attitude is the software of employability.

I will share here regarding the art part of employability in detail and the science part of skills and knowledge to less extent, totally based on my own experience and observation of my direct reportees in the last 30 years. I will be providing my perspective from completely practical experience I had and no theory. Align it to your specific situation, if need be.

1. ATTITUDES ESSENTIAL FOR EMPLOYABILITY OF AN INDIVIDUAL

TREAT YOUR JOB AS YOUR 'OWN' BUSINESS

You must act as if you are the owner and every activity you do on the job must be done with cent percent commitment and dedication. It shows up in your results.

If you have promised your boss that you will complete a certain task by particular time, it has to be done. As an example, there were times in my career, I completed my marketing presentation assignments and delivered the presentation CD at my boss's house at midnight as he has to catch an early morning flight. Over a period of time I had cultivated an image that if something is assigned to me and the deadline is fixed, it will be delivered in almost all the cases except when things are beyond my control.

CONTRIBUTE MINIMUM 10X RETURNS TO YOUR COMPANY

You are aware about your CTC (Cost To Company) and you must try and provide a minimum 10X value to the company. In sales and marketing jobs, it is easily measurable in terms of business generated but in other functions like Operations, Finance, Admin, Distribution, Training and Development or R&D, you have to develop your own metrics to deliver 10X value to the company.

BE ADAPTABLE AND FLEXIBLE TO DIFFERENT TYPES OF SITUATIONS

Those people who are resilient in approach but firmly focused on their goals in their jobs are found to be highly successful and are always in demand in the job market. Those people who follow rigid practices without understanding that the world around them is changing the ways to conduct the job also would ultimately become outdated and unsuccessful in their assignments and will become irrelevant to the job market.

The key to success in constantly changing scenarios is changing self, upgrading skills and knowledge as per changed situations in the company or industry or change of bosses or change of company culture or companies' strategies. I have seen when a new boss takes over many employees cannot adjust and either leave or are asked to go. Also, I have seen some people after getting the job, unable to adjust to the new company work environment or new company culture. Your employability greatly depends on adaptability to new situations, new company cultures and systems, new bosses and new peer pressures.

SELECT SMALL PART OF YOUR JOB AND BECOME IRREPLACEABLE IN THAT AREA

Whichever department or function you are in, there will be always some key areas to the final outcome. Identify those areas which are absolutely essential for the success of the activity or project or company then master that one area by whichever means possible, may be taking training, coaching or acquiring a specific skill.

SELF-CONFIDENCE, PERSISTENCE AND GRIT

I have seen a lot of talented people fail just because they are not self-confident. Even I was a victim of this syndrome but over a period of time I have overcome it. Self-confident people will shine in most of the situations at work but one should be careful that you should not cross a thin line of over-confidence, then the decline will start.

One more trait of a person that I found very essential for succeeding in these hyper competition times is persistence and grit.

Above 5 important attitudinal aspects I have seen in most of the successful people at work. So, to remain employable, one should cultivate these winning attitudes.

2. PRACTICAL DOMAIN KNOWLEDGE

Whatever may be your domain, you need to have relevant knowledge related –
- Your particular industry
- Competition and other companies operating in the domain
- Technical, Geographical, Political, Social and Economic situations
- Your own company
- The functional departments with whom you have to work closely
- Related to your own job function

3. ESSENTIAL SKILLS IN CURRENT SITUATION

The two aspects of employability discussed are very crucial but the skills required to do a job are non-negotiable and you should possess them. When it comes to skills many people may be equal but winning attitudes and right knowledge will ensure you are ahead in the game of employability.

So, let's take stock of skills required to be employable, in general.
- Technical skills related to a particular job
- Communication – upward, downward and sideways, oral and written
- Team building skills
- Interpersonal skills
- Selling skills – selling ideas or goods, within company or outside company
- Ability to solve problems as they arise
- Decision making – Most important at senior levels
- Strategic thinking – Essential for long term sustenance and growth
- Multitasking – Ability to do many things at time has become important as multiple things are involved in a job

- Result orientation – Ensuring desired outcomes has become an important skill in today's dynamic and hyper competitive world
- Time management – Prioritizing, Delegation, Scheduling,
- Implementation skills
- Documentation – You should have excellent record keeping skills, maybe you can use many software available for that

TAKE HOME MESSAGE

Continuous employability is a big challenge today considering the industry scale disruptions happening and virtually every industry is getting impacted with rapid changes in new age technologies like artificial intelligence, machine learning, robots, increased penetration of smartphones and internet, short business life cycles, rapidly changing economic and environment scenarios.

To remain employable, one has to keep themselves updated in all three major areas I have discussed in this chapter- Winning Attitudes, Updated and upgraded knowledge and upskilling.

AKASH LOKHANDE

Akash Lokhande is an Employability Coach and Soft skills trainer with experience of 4 years in the training industry. He is on a mission to help youth to get employable. He works with them on different skills so that they can overcome any problem in life as well as in their career.

ARTICLE ON EMPLOYABILITY

Recently I came across a news that in May 2020, 30 Cr jobs are in danger due to COVID-19 pandemic in India. We must understand it is almost 30% of India's population.

It is a huge risk for India as well. Can we prevent this?

Many of the people have already lost their jobs and are really struggling.

Many people are still working and some of them are already on the verge of getting fired. They should really prove to their company that they are the asset for their company.

Being an Employability Expert I have spoken to some industry people and discussed this situation.

The key point of discussion was how can an employee prevent himself from getting fired?

Work from Home: - Those who are currently working, most of them are doing work from home. Some of the people who are working from home are really not serious about it. They simply don't know what is expected from them while working from home. I observed some people and I realized most of them are taking it very lightly and they are simply wasting their time.

They must realize that they can lose their job at any point of time. Some companies already have fired 3rd party staffing and people who were on contract. Company would not hesitate to fire non-productive employees as well.

While working from home the first thing we should take care is 'being on time'. Because most of the time seniors may have eye on people who are following their time. Every company has different parameters to check the productivity of an employee. Some choose screen timing, some depend on login and logout timing and meetings after it, and some companies are task oriented, they assign a task to an employee and checks whether he completed it. Irrespective of any method company chooses it is expected that work has to be done effectively.

Being flexible: – As I was having a discussion with one of my friends, he was telling the advantages of doing 'Work from Home'. He said that people are saving a couple of hours of traveling as they don't need to go out and travel. Earlier what used to happen was after traveling this much nobody wanted to open their laptops and work even when any issue arrived. They would try to solve it on the next day once they reached office. Now what is happening is whenever there is an issue there is someone who is there to resolve it. So, companies can ask someone to work in different shifts or if an employee is asked to do something, though it is not their responsibility, they are expected to take care of it. What I want to say here is employees should not complain. If they can do it, they must do it.

Increasing involvement: – While doing work from home companies are continuously in communication with employees through emails and messages. What often people do is they ignore the messages they receive. It can be because either employee is really very busy in delivering his task or he is pretending that he is busy. This is really very unprofessional to ignore the messages.

What I would suggest is that employees must get involved in this communication process. It also shows that he/she is paying close attention to all the tasks. It shows that the employee is connected with the team. Here it is a chance to get connected with seniors or top leadership so that you can also understand the strategy and contribute to your full potential. You can gain the attention by proving you are ready to take the next step of your ladder.

Everybody hates showing off, but these are the circumstances where you really need to tell your team that how hard you are working, and you are delivering on time. Because No company wants to lay off a person who listens carefully and delivers as expected.

Learning a new skill or Sharpening the old one: – Those who are still working with any company must understand that if a company has still kept them it means they have certain skill sets which company wants and others are lacking. In these circumstances people are getting a lot of time because of 'work for home'.

Everybody has his/her own way to spend his free time. What I observed is some people are always obsessed with learning new things. So some people can choose which skill to learn. But this is not the case with everyone.

Some people are not so interested in learning a new skill so I would suggest here is that they can sharpen their skills that they already possess. By this they will stay in the race and can perform to a level which is expected from them. It is not always all about how fast you can learn new things, sometimes it is about how you can make use of your existing skill set.

REKHA VAGHELA

Rekha Vaghela is a Relationship Counselor and Human Values Parenting Coach. She found her purpose after working for more than 13+ years in Human Resource Management. She worked for top brands like Piramal Healthcare Group and India Medtronic Pvt. Ltd. She is on a Mission to connect with people in different ways like Parents to Children, Life Partners and of course connecting to Inner self.

HOW I DISCOVERED 9 SECRETS (PRINCIPLES) OF JOYFUL PARENTING?

There is enough literature available on Parenting Style, Child psychology, Adult behavior and many more related topics. What Parents need to learn is how to become a right match for their child as each child is unique with distinct needs. How to be wiser towards their way of life? How to be capable of being able to guide and lead them to live a fulfilling life with contentment?

Today the challenges our children encounter are increasing at the nano speed of technology upgradation. The frequency and intensity of day to day challenges are beyond the purview of parents as they never know how to cope up with them. This is for sure, children cannot be handled the same way we were, by our parents. But the real problem is, there isn't a standard manual or guidelines which parents can refer to and prepare well in advance.

After a successful corporate career in Learning and Development for more than 13 years working with MNCs in healthcare industries, I took a sabbatical to spend time with my children in 2014. During that period, I discovered my passion to add value in the life of Parents. I remember 6 years back when I took the charge as a full time Mother, my situation was similar like today "How COVID -19 has made all of us – Self Reliant & Self Aware?"

But I see a huge difference in the way I handled the situation now and then in 2014. Being a mother of two growing children – teenage son and pre-teen daughter has helped me to look at the challenges of parents with more empathy. I want to share here that COVID-19 has taught me more about myself and my children too. I see that I have become more patient, understanding and engaging with my children through various activities at home. I am able to do more work during lockdown with extra energy and stretching myself to do many additional tasks without external help but yes with encouraging support from family members. I learnt children have a lot of talent and need to be nurtured with love and patience.

However, the situation may not be true for all the parents. I have interacted with a couple of parents who have found this change unpleasant and not sure how to manage work, children and family priorities.

Few common challenges mentioned by parents are the same during COVID -19 and before also. There is excessive screen time, discipline, study habits and behavioral issues like too much dependence on parents which has made children lethargic, ignoring their physical, social, emotional and overall wellbeing.

I have been offering many programs to help parents to handle above challenges. Some of the programs which were found useful by parents are:
- *3As of Digital Era Parenting,*
- *9 Parenting Principles*
- *How to raise an Emotionally Intelligent Child?*

Most of the parents know a lot of information about Parenting but they miss out on "How to apply and practice them?"

I would like to share my journey of connecting with children. This will support parents to adopt a consistent approach to raise children in a nurturing environment. My recommendations are based on my philosophy of Life and distinctive concept of Human Parenting Values.

Each parent needs to understand basic Parenting principles to raise children who are responsible, matured and independent. To practice these principles, learn 3As of Digital Era Parenting, which can be applied by each parent irrespective of the age of their child.

1st A: Accept the Children As They Are
2nd A: Acknowledge Child's Presence in Your Life
3rd A: Appreciate Their Thoughts/Ideas.

I am mentioning a few practical steps in this direction. I trust that our common goal is to see our children thrive and live their life to their fullest potential as a Human being.

I am well aware that Parenting is a big responsibility and it needs constant awareness.

As the child needs education, parents too are required to learn new attitudes and activities to enhance parenting skills which will enable them to build joyful relationships with children. I have briefly covered challenges of today's parents and few ideas to handle them.

I want to define Values / Attributes as a PARENT need to demonstrate to raise children.
P- Patience
A – Acceptance
R – Responsible
E – Empathy
N- Nurturing
T – Trust

How to demonstrate Patience when a child is always demanding and not understanding?
I remember how my son used to behave adamantly for new things when friends got it in school or latest things shown in the movies / screen. I had crazy situations and was not aware of "How to say No" when demands like branded items only for sports activities, technologytoys &gadgets, pokémoncards, watch, perfumes, movies, eating junk food frequently etc.

I learnt to set limits and manage emotional tantrums when my children were getting angry/shouted for unfulfilled demands. Some of them are:
- *Excessive Mobile /TV time*
- *Misbehavior with Sibling / Children in society & school*
- *More entertainment time v/s completing studies*

I learnt to **Accept** the child, when he/she showed disrespect through words and actions. I discovered that when my children behaved inappropriately, it called for my deeper attention and connection with them to understand the unfulfilled demand of Love and Respect. When you observe a child showing any of the following behavior or emotional tantrums, bring Love & Empathy in your approach.

- *Behaving adamant/stubborn (not listening)*
- *Failure in studies*
- *Lack of interest in particular subject*
- *Distraction towards mobile / technology*

I learnt, I need to show *Responsible behavior (Accountable/answerable /in charge/in control/Authority)* towards children with a balance of Love and Law using **WATCH.**

- Words
- Actions
- Thoughts
- Character
- Heart

I learnt to be *Resilient (Flexible)* towards children without compromising the discipline rules and my authority. To do this, I discovered, parent need following traits:

- *Assertive communication*
- *Clear understanding between both spouses about handling child's behavior*
- *Hidden meaning behind each behavior. Remember a child has motive & purpose when interacting with you. Like adults have when they connect with people.*

I learnt to show *Nurturing* through love and my presence in their life:

- *When the child has emotional outburst with anyone*
- *When the child has an important event to perform ie. exam / competition*

I learnt to show *Trust* in my child's capability. It is the key for successful relationships and emotional bonding with children.

- *Allow child to explore various interest areas*
- *Give experiences to learn from different events in life*
- *Motivate children to venture and pursue new hobbies.*
- *Best way to get cooperation is to partner with them wherever possible.*

To develop all of the above traits, each parent requires genuine interest in the child's overall development and skills like win-win negotiation and positive firmness to make things happen. This looks challenging in the modern world as priorities and the role of parents has changed.

VIJAYALAKSHMI RAMAN

Vijayalakshmi Raman is an MBB with data science in mind. With 2 decades of experience in multiple domains, she wishes to help the working women manage their work life balance and to find that extra time for personal development which would make them 25% more productive than now within 6 months which would pave way for earning more recognition, recommendations and an increased paycheck.

LOCK DOWN:
IMPACT ON PHARMACEUTICAL DOMAIN

PANDEMIC AND ITS ACCEPTANCE

Change is the one thing which is new normal, Change is the only thing which does not change.

While we are looking at the pandemic as an uninvited guest, let's go past that and look at the real scenario.

This pandemic has taught us all to work from home, has built in the extra discipline within us.

We are in a bit more responsible place to take care of our physical health, mental health and financial health.

Approaches will be more into the human level.

People have to be available online henceforth, so the video etiquette, public speaking and behavioral styles have to be learnt well. Mentoring and training also will become digital and we should be ready to accept the remote learning trend.

In short, we all need a great Digital Transformation with a shift in mindset to cope up with the organizational and operational change.

Because it's always "80% mindset and 20% Skills" as Dev Gadhvi says with ref to pareto principle.

Hence, we all have come together in search of our inner niche and are associated with JJ's Community.

DOMAIN VISION

"It has before, it will again" that's the power of science. When science wins, we all win, says Pfizer.

"It's an exciting new era in medicine," says Novartis.

"It's ship will have come in with a package bearing the Golden Ticket" was the comment of John Lamattina in Stat news while speaking about Big Pharma.

Pharmaceutical domain as such is in its all-time different level, right from the basic supply of masks until the export of hydroxychloroquine to our neighboring countries to cure the pandemic effects.

COMPANIES WHICH ARE HIRING NOW.

Source Name: Recruit.net

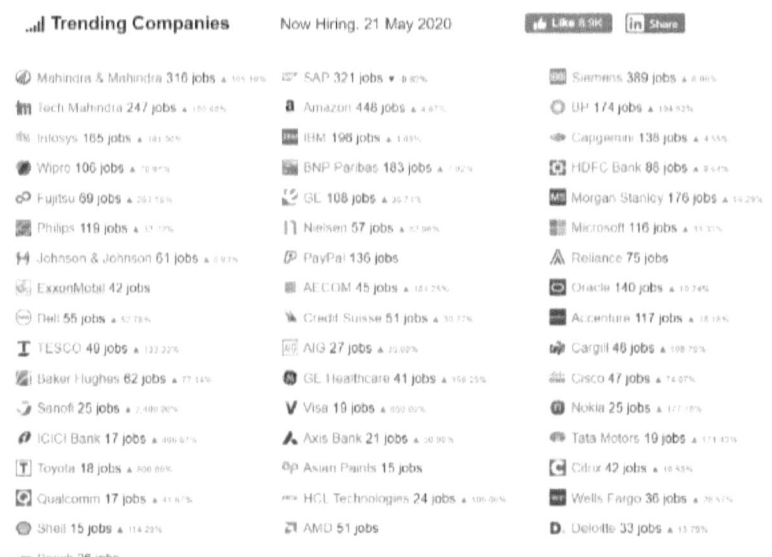

What is in store for the job seeker?

We are going to experience a new changed working structure. The more flexible you are the more you will be sought after.

Your attitude and qualities will be looked into before the skillset, since skillset can be taught.

Not just that, since work from home culture has become a success, there are going to be more new roles, new teachings and new learnings.

Be the passionate you and go with the flow.

What are the actions we can expect from an employer?

Employers would downsize the company area but not the employees

As there are lot of talks going on, there is going to be a pay-out system as per demand.

Would reduce travel plans, business visa applications to only those very important visits.

Would look in various ways and means to maximize earnings.

How can experienced persons like me contribute to the new normal?

Try and upskill as much as possible and be adaptive to the changing culture of the company.

Be a role model and show the juniors that we are all capable of being our best at any given point of time.

As Maxwell says in Psycho Cybernetics, let's all use our creative mechanism to learn, practice and experience new habits of thinking, imagining, remembering and acting to create a new self-image, bringing success and happiness by achieving our goals.

While there will be a lot of hit financially for the companies due to lockdown, let us use lean management in cutting out the 7 wastes at this point of time.

Not just that let us identify those projects which can potentially help our organization to save by means of improvement, process reengineering and so on.

Let's accept for the implementation of more Bots which would evolve freeing up to perform new roles.

This would also help the company save money and to bring in more work (More work = more money)

Do's and Don'ts – The new rule book

Do's

Be proactive and be the solution. Keep learning every day.
Have a positive mindset and attitude.
Help who are in need of your knowledge, teach and train and be a guiding light.

Don'ts

Don't be unhygienic.
Don't be that rebellious selfish person, you'll be left alone.
Don't become a frog in that well.

SAI BHASKAR

Sai Bhaskar is a Career Planning Facilitator and Study Abroad Consultant with over 2 decades of experience in IT Industry. He is on a mission to help students identify their career goals and progressively help them achieve the same. Sai is also on a mission to help at least 50,000 people gain employability skills in the next 5 years. To achieve this goal, Sai would like to collaborate with individuals and institutions that can provide employability training in various sectors and thus enable employability skill development of the young workforce.

This chapter is the intellectual property of Sai Bhasker and he/she retains the sole and unhindered right to use/ modify/ repurpose/ adapt/ reformat the contents at his/ her pleasure. No other individual/ entity, including the publisher possesses any rights whatsoever over the content published in this book under a particular author's name.

POST LOCKDOWN: NIOS AS AN OPTION TO IMPROVE EMPLOYABILITY

National level COVID-19 lockdown resulted in a drastic change to the education system in India and especially to the K-12 sector. Many schools and teachers have adapted to the online medium of teaching and the same was well received by parents and students. I am sure that the situation gave an opportunity to parents to better understand the potential skills & interests of the child as they were watching them learn at home.

Based on this experience and keeping in mind the need to develop employability skills as well as help students pursue their passion, parents should take a look at NIOS (National Institute of Open Schooling) as an education stream for their children. NIOS has a flexible system as well as provides an opportunity for students to spend their time learning topics that they are very much interested in and that can help them shape their careers.

NIOS is safe for children who may not be able to fit into the regular school post lockdown due to their own health restrictions. In such situations, parents may opt to enroll them into NIOS and help the child learn from home through free resources provided by the Government which also makes it more affordable. If the parent is keen to help the child get prepared for various competitive exams, then they can plan to engage a private tutor to handle classes at the time convenient for the child. NIOS is recognized and promoted by MHRD which is a Government body and hence students can get admission to reputed colleges/universities of their choice in the future.

Affordability, Safety, Recognition and anything else that you're expecting from a board of education is possible through NIOS. As many parents would have identified what their child is passionate about and where they see them in future using their skill/knowledge, need to start working through this process.

A group of parents in a particular vicinity with similar interests could start sharing the responsibility of guiding and mentoring these students periodically by enrolling them into the appropriate online programs. This will help develop a healthy social life as you're frequently meeting likeminded families and watching each other's kid grow confident and happy.

Moreover, this gives an opportunity to passionate and educated members of the community who are interested to help kids learn with an earning opportunity by taking care of the learning needs of the students.

For example:

a set of students who are interested in a particular sport / dance / art can join together and practice on a regular basis. They can also engage a renowned & experienced coach across the globe that will be able to help them learn the skills needed through an online medium. As they do this, they can also enroll into an online coaching that provides them the necessary academics classes as per NIOS syllabus OR an entrance exam for which they want to get prepared.

As the students will avoid several tasks that consume time and energy when they have to travel for long distances to school, they will have more time to pursue their passion as well as spend this time to learn employable skills that will help them have a better career in future.

SAHIL MALHOTRA

*Solving problems for customers and their supply chains primarily using Data Analysis & Data Visualization, and reporting these insights to strategic decision making teams across industries, sectors and organizations is something **Sahil Malhotra** is passionate about.*

IMPORTANCE OF SUPPLY CHAINS IN COVID

Supply Chains – I believe everyone knows something about these. To reiterate, supply chains are the link between suppliers, manufacturers, distributors, wholesalers, retailers, and customers/end consumers. But is it as simple as this? On the theoretical side, this looks simple! But when we look at the variables and factors involved, it is quite intricate and complex.

In this piece, I am primarily taking insights from the Deloitte Report* and other articles* which I accessed primarily using Google search.

As of today, Thursday, May 21, 2020 the impact of the COVID virus is that approx. 5.1 Million people have been affected by the deadly virus with India reporting 112,000 cases per se.

The virus has not only disrupted supply chains but also has compelled us to think not just as supply chain managers and professionals but also as a civilization. Let us come to the numbers later but as of May 21, 2020 there have been innumerable number of businesses failing, people filing unemployment claims where such claims give some reliefs or benefits to the claimants, furloughs and layoffs, loss in demand of products or services, and last but not least rise in inventories as there have been negligent deliveries especially in April 2020.

From the Indian perspective, there were almost zero new Automotive and Durable sales (in April 2020) as everything was shut down due to nationwide lockdown. What about housing supply chain? The number of housing units available for sale versus the number sold only increased during these times. The only supply chain unaffected to a large extent was the food-and-food products supply chain with companies in these sectors actually performing somewhat during these times.

But still can we easily say that the food supply chain also did not witness any disruption per se? Not really! The products that comprise the food supply chain – groceries (esp. dry groceries), FMCG (fast-moving consumer goods) items among others also did face a demand degrowth.

Were we as consumers able to get all the usual brands and items under these brands in stores where we frequented to buy such items during this period? If this supply chain was not disrupted as much, then why did we witness this situation where we sometimes saw retailers running out of stocks of our favorite Maggi noodles, for instance?

The reason that can be one among others is unavailability of last-mile deliveries from the wholesalers/distributors to the retail outlets where we go buy these groceries/staples (not including the grocery deliveries we may order online). As we saw the lockdown gaining momentum, the service providers such as truckers ended up having no drivers or staff to load these vehicles from the warehouses/distribution centers and then dispatching the orders to retailers. In addition, as the virus created chaos, there was more disruption and panic which set in rather than some sanity gaining momentum in these times.

THE COVID NUMBERS GAME

Let's look at some numbers before we move forward with possible mitigation mechanisms or measures for disrupted supply chains.

185 countries have been affected by this virus as of Apr 30, 2020.

Dow Jones and FTSE witnessed their biggest drops (Quarterly) in indices since 1987, with FTSE 100 falling -25% and Dow Jones falling -19% as of April 27, 2020.

More than 30 M people in the US alone filed for unemployment benefits as of Apr 30, 2020.

Apr 27, 2020 also witnessed Brent crude trade at $20.59 a barrel, its lowest level in 21 years with another incredible situation wherein the US oil prices turned negative for the first time, trading at $(37.63) as of Apr 27, 2020.

As per estimates, advanced economies such as – Canada, France, Germany, Italy, Japan, UK, US are expected to hit recession in 2020 – all contracting 5% or lower.

Not to mean it literally, the icing on the cake is the hit faced by the Travel and Tourism industry with more than 100 countries imposing restrictions on both – inbound and outbound tourism traffic.

As per estimates from the World Travel and Tourism Council, 75 million jobs are at stake (globally) in addition to a revenue loss of $2.1 Trillion. Not to mention, the tourism industry is not only a job generator but also a foreign exchange earner.

SOME POSSIBLE MEASURES

Given the scenario prevalent due to the COVID 19 situation, there are certain measures which need due attention from a supply chain perspective before its time that we face another disruption of a similar magnitude. *Resilience* is the need of the hour as far as the contemporary global supply chains are concerned.

Supply chain visibility, Digitization, and Blockchain are some of the possible mechanisms proposed by none other than the WEF (World Economic Forum). WEF states and I quote – "Companies who sell finished goods generally know production and shipment schedules for their Tier 1 suppliers, but they usually have little to no knowledge of suppliers further up the chain."

In supply chains, such situations usually occur due to lack of supply chain visibility. This visibility is not only important during normal times but also it becomes vital for survival esp. during times of crises such as COVID 19. Visibility not only leads to efficient supply chains but also has the ability to provide the much-needed agility to these chains.

In Supply chain parlance, the lack of visibility leads to a phenomenon popularly known as the "Bullwhip effect". This is one of the most important issues in any supply chain arising primarily due to the lack of visibility in supply chains. Generally, the Bullwhip effect is a situation where there is an increase in the order variability within a supply chain. The higher a particular supply chain stakeholder is in a supply chain, the higher is the order variability.

Any organization which encounters this phenomenon can mitigate its impact by not only improving the information flow but also improving the (supply chain) partners' cooperation within supply chains.

Practical cases cited by the WEF include – Fiat Chrysler Automobiles, which announced mid-Feb 2020 that it would be halting production at a car factory in Serbia as it could not get parts from China, Hyundai made a similar announcement for factories in Korea.

Supply chain visibility across the value chain can be achieved using one or more of the following –

1. **From paperwork to Digitization** – COVID19 protective measures have ensured that operations dependent on physical assets (paperwork) can face serious bottlenecks like in present times;

2. **Data Privacy for suppliers** – Loss of commercial advantage to upstream suppliers stops them from revealing information to their end customers, a problem solved when Blockchains are used.

3. **Supplier Incentives to share Data** – Data is information – there may be buyers who value data and may consider paying the suppliers for the data itself in addition to the goods they source from the suppliers.

4. **Start Now** – Don't assume such disruptions may not repeat themselves – Spot On! Usually supply chain initiatives come with their respective lead times. An effective move at present would be to roll out supply chain finance programs to support financially weak suppliers to make the value chain capital efficient.

Absolutely, as I complete this piece there is another natural calamity which has already hit us in the Indian subcontinent – the cyclone Amphan hitting India has already started causing destruction in West Bengal and parts of Odisha. In addition to taking 72 lives till today, the cyclone has also misplaced a few hundred thousand people already from their domiciles.

SRIIDHAR KALYANARAMAN

Sriidhar Kalyanaraman *(SKR) is the Founder of "SKR School of Financial Fitness" and "SKR Financial Freedom Hub" aimed at providing right financial education for every Indian.*
SKR is on a mission to impact a Million lives positively during his lifetime.

MAKING INDIANS FINANCIALLY FIT

The missing puzzle in formal education today is right financial education which I am trying to cover in this book in a simple and concise manner for every Indian to understand in simple language and form.

Earning money is just one piece of the puzzle. How well we plan our finances will decide our financial future.

We Plan, Prepare, Practice and Perform for things like family vacations to give the best experience to our family with best interest in our mind for our families, but how many of us plan and prepare for emergencies which is not in anybody's control.

"Formal education will earn you a living, self-education will make you a fortune" - Jim Rohn.

Increasing immunity will save us from pandemic, likewise financial fitness will save us from exigencies

"Never depend on single income, create multiple streams to survive and thrive in this competitive world"

UNTOLD MONEY SECRETS DEMYSTIFIED

Top 3 Secrets about money:
1) Don't buy the things which you don't need, to impress the people you don't like, with the money you don't have
2) Don't put all your eggs in one basket
3) Don't do the same thing again and again and expect different results

Budget Framework:
Emergency Funds- Keep 6-12 months of funds in your account to access any point in time which includes {(Rent, mortgage, bills, food etc.,}

EMERGENCY FUNDS USED WHEN INCOME STOPS TEMPORARILY FOR ONE OR MANY REASONS AS BELOW

- Job loss
- Ill health of self
- Taking care of family member
- Sabbatical
- Loss of income
- Any pandemic like COVID-19

Income – Savings = Expenses

Savings must be your first expense/EMI from your account. (We will discuss the various avenues for long term savings in detail in asset classes division below)

50:30:20 is a thumb rule to follow which will save us from any financial disaster

"No one size fits all"

- 50% towards needs of family (rent,mortgage,bills,food, children education)
- 30% towards wants of family (eating out, family trips, to buy things we enjoy)
- 20% towards long term savings (retirement planning which will be discussed)

Goal planning:

Goals are defined as -

- Short Term Goals: 6 months – 1 year (Example - Purchase of TV, Phone,Vehicle etc.)
- Medium Term Goals: 2- 3 years (Downpayment of house, Foreign Vacation, buy Car)
- Long Term Goals: 7 years and above (children education, retirement)

Investment in various asset classes will help you attain your goals faster and easier.

Note- Risk appetite is critically important to understand for yourself before choosing any investment in any asset class.

VARIOUS ASSET CLASSES

Commonly known asset classes among people are–
- Gold
- Real estate
- Deposits

Other Asset classes available–
- Stocks/Equities – Shares of company
- Bonds – Bonds issued by government and corporates
- Mutual funds – equity funds, index funds, liquid funds, debt funds

Before choosing any asset class check–
- Return on investment
- Risk to reward ratio
- Liquidity
- Risk involved

Risk Planning–
- Life insurance
- Health Insurance
- Home Insurance

"Protection is better than cure".

Understand the terms and conditions properly and choose the right ones which ensure and covers all risks.

Insurance acts as a protection in case of uncertain events that may occur in our lives.

Insurance is a must in majority of the cases as it is the only vehicle which helps our families protect from financial stress due to death of a breadwinner, disabilities, sickness, calamities that may occur which is truly unpredictable.

Investment Planning-

- Investment planning has to be done basis goals (short,medium,long) as discussed above and choose from the various asset class available mentioned above and considering risk appetite.
- Short term- Deposits, Liquid funds, savings bank account are better
- Medium term- Debt funds, bonds are better
- Long term- Equity mutual funds, index funds, stocks, gold etc. can be considered.

Retirement Planning:

Retirement planning is a long-term goal and earlier the plan the sooner the retirement as compounding is the eighth wonder of the world and works magic which will be explained below.

Follow the guidelines in the long-term goal planning and the asset class described in investment planning which is mentioned above

Tax Planning:

Plan your taxes using the most out of 80C, 80CCC, 80CCD (1), 80D This keeps changing mostly every year with the finance ministry budget and hence plan accordingly by using the section available applicable to you.

Estate Planning:

- Protect your loved ones by making legally binding will planning/succession planning to ensure smooth transfer of assets.
- Will/Succession planning will help avoid
- Family disputes
- Guardianship of minor children
- Nomination for assets

Passive Income:
Passive income is generated by not working actively but earnings generated via assets in the form of conventional and digital form which is detailed below

Conventional method of passive income-
- Rental income
- Interest on deposits
- Dividends from stock/bonds
- Royalties from books/music etc.

New age streams of passive income -
- Affiliate marketing
- Blogging
- Influencer marketing on YouTube, Instagram etc.
- Online course creation
- E-books
- 5x returns using rental properties by listing on Airbnb, hotel sites etc.
- Undertaking freelance works using specific skills

Compounding is the eighth wonder of the world and works magic
15,000 invested for 15 years @ 15% (CAGR) = 1 crore
15,000 invested for 30 years @ 15 % (CAGR)= 10 Crore

"If you are born poor it's not your mistake, if you die poor it's your mistake"

"Never say I can't afford it, instead ask yourself how can I afford it" it will open possibilities and work wonders for you as everything comes with mindset, discipline and habits.

ARINJAY RAJJ

Arinjay Rajj is a National faculty of Art of living foundation and State council member of Youth leadership training program with 20 years of experience in the field of positive psychology, yoga and meditation. He is also a Harvard medical school certified expert in coping with the stress of COVID. He is on a mission to educate and instill empowering belief systems in youth by raising their self-worth to achieve success and fulfillment in their life.

HOW TO ELEVATE YOUR SELF-WORTH POST COVIDCRISIS

Seeing through a lens of possibility even in the midst of adversity helps in exploring the new version of ourselves and new possibilities which are otherwise not possible. We all know that the human mind tends to cling to negativity, and at times of crisis we start feeling like the bad is stronger than good.

At these times it becomes important to become aware of our patterns and deliberately put attention to visualize the possibilities that surround us, and at the same time being grateful for what we have lived so far. Most of us believe that we need to be extraordinary to come out of this struggling life. It's because we forget that small meaningful and massive action taken consistently can solve the most wicked problems, we face to achieve our dreams and desires.

We are truly active interpreters of things happening around us, and if we are not aligned to our positive mindset then obviously by our active interpretation, we will not see any worth or significance of experiences life throws at us in challenging times. So, at times when so many things are coming to us that cause fear and anxiety, we need to focus on getting our positive emotions in sync with their meaning and purpose in life. This gives us hope and opens up new possibilities.

We need to combine all our available resources be it mental, physical or emotional to design the framework and set things in the right perspective. The purpose of our life often changes during the tragic events of life during some disaster or after the loss of loved ones. We often ponder on a life purpose post hardship. This is the perfect time to reexamine our dreams and desires, whether they need to be too materialistic or self-referral identity is what we need at the end of the day. Now is the time to rebuild our purpose on what matters the most now.

In hard times our greatest strength comes from the power of within. It's about how we perceive about ourselves and what affects our ability to bounce back, adapt, reconnect and transform challenges into opportunities for bringing out the new version of ourselves.

But the question is how do we elevate ourselves especially when the road uphill seems to be dark and clueless. It is very obvious to get disillusioned if we frequently get overwhelmed by stress factors that lead us to doubt our ability to face challenges and overcome them.

In difficult times we can feel very depleted and find it challenging to survive, and the best way to thrive rather than survive is to manage our energy. We need to uplift our state of existence by practicing some daily rituals every day to increase the probability of having good energy and vitality. We need energy to grow, learn and become vibrant in our surroundings.

So, to start with we all know our sleeping patterns can be disrupted in challenging and stressful times. But we should try to get a maximum 7-8 hours of sleep, and it's possible if you follow the routine of going to bed every day at the same time. During the day we can observe and audit our energy levels, if we can identify which thing gives us more energy and which takes it away then we may have a ready blueprint of where to focus more.

There is a natural tendency to focus on failure difficulties and challenges, fortunately there is a very powerful tool to cope up with these problems and to focus on our collective consciousness and that is to identify what's going right in our life and what's going good in the world, and feeling sense of gratitude for all of it.

Expressing gratitude directly impacts our health and happiness. Different research studies have proved that practicing gratitude can help build strong immunity among many psychological and physical benefits. So, gratitude matters. It helps us become physically, emotionally and mentally healthier especially in challenging times. When it is easy to focus on negativity and challenges, then consciously replacing it with gratefulness helps us to emerge better off in the time of crisis.

Now it's very important to understand the very powerful human principle of reciprocity. If you help someone and he also helps you in return then this is called reciprocity in practice. You help me and I help you, but this is not always the most powerful form of reciprocal activity.

Sometimes you don't get help from the person you have helped before, but you get help from an unexpected source. This also happens because of the energy you have given to someone; it comes back to you through different forms and channels.

And requesting for this help becomes a catalyst and drives the receiving process to you. Nothing happens without you asking for the help. Nobody is going to read your mind and tell you what you need.

The biggest block of asking for the help is your assumptions of what people will feel about your competency and weakness. but on the contrary, research says that as long as you make thoughtful, intelligent requests, people will think you as more competent in your area of expertise.

Today at the times of global crisis, it becomes more critical to reach out and ask for what you need. It could be emotional support or helping hands or anything, but please understand no one can help you unless you ask, and when you ask you realize that people are more generous to help. So at these times it becomes imperative for us to look for opportunities to help people, and also please feel free to ask for the help if you need it. Both are equally important.

Elevating self-worth means those positive psychological changes that happen in us as we go through challenging times. Sometimes the hardships really challenge the belief system we carry, and as we struggle through the challenging times, we are basically rebuilding a new belief system and assumptions which motivates us even in strange times. And through this process change happens, growth happens and finally it transforms us in our new versions. And as a result of this, our relationship with our family and near and dear ones improves.

Secondly, we learn to build our financial framework around the things we love and are passionate about. We discover our own strength and the power of resilience. Dark times are a great opportunity to create a new you to elevate your self-worth.

Stay safe and be blessed!

PRASHANT KESHAV

Prashant *(Founder at Career Buddy) is an MBA, Certified Career Coach from ICF (USA), Employability expert, and author of an upcoming book "Be the CEO of your Career". With over 15 Years of experience in Telecom, Retail and Education Industry, he is on a mission to empower students and professionals to design a career which they enjoy pursuing, find a job they love and earn what they deserve.*

I AM WRITING MY SECOND HALF @40

It was in the year 2018, and I remember the date precisely, 25th February. I was sitting with two of my very dear friends in café coffee day at Vashi, Mumbai and asked each other 'Why do we do, what do we do'?

Was it because of pure interest in our work or was it just because of peer pressure, family pressure, society pressure or to prove ourselves in the eyes of others?

For most of us, our career was hardly guided by any interest in it but more to do with chasing ambition, designation and earning a plethora of money.

That answer changed everything.

Over a period of time, I realized it was not only me but the majority of the people who I spoke to, did not have a convincing answer about "why do they, what they do?" and they lacked career direction.

Perhaps it was too late to go back in time for ourselves, but we saw an opportunity to ensure that succeeding generations have a convincing answer to the question, 'Why do they do what they do?' so that they can design a career which is happy, fulfilling and profitable over a long period of time.

I had some ideas which were vague and scattered, but was not sure of how to get started.

It was August, 2018, when I came in contact with Jogesh Jain whom I fondly call "Sir ji" because of deep respect. He not only brought clarity but also raised my belief level that I can offer my knowledge and experience, make an impact and build business around it. "Career Buddy" an idea & thought, was born one and half years ago, during his mentorship period.

As time progressed, there was always creative tension inside me that wanted me to quit my job and follow my passion to help every Prashant who lacked a convincing answer of 'why do they do what they do?' and career direction.

It was in February, 2020, when I finally decided to quit my job and started working aggressively on my start-up called "Career Buddy". Till a year back, it was just a thought and it is now a reality.

It is born out of an audacious dream to help students and professionals be better equipped to make a career choice they enjoy pursuing and offer customized career solutions for every career need at different stages of their career that are unique to each individual for their career success.

We are on a path to impact the lives of 1 lakh + students and professionals by 2025.

At Career Buddy, we leverage our vast and varied corporate experience; most reliable Career psychometric assessment tool and proprietary 4D framework (Discover, Design, Develop & Destination) to help professionals and college graduates to plan and develop careers that are profitable in all aspects.

This 4D framework has been constructed from the research which I have done by studying books, from my own corporate experience and speaking to various students and professionals in the last couple of years. It has helped over 100 professionals to gain competitive advantage in their career.

We are so proud of this framework which we have constructed and hope that it will help scores of people to fulfil their career potential by becoming the CEO of their own career.

In my fifteen years of corporate career, I have realized that most of the people are stuck in a job to pay their bills month on month basis that give little or no satisfaction.

But, when we transition from job to calling, the entire game changes. I realize that it is worth it, to do what you love to do. It takes time; it is a long-drawn process. You fail, you win, you fail, you win and the cycle keeps going. On the way, you will doubt yourself, your actions and your beliefs. But if you persist you will reach where you are meant to reach. Don't give up!

Listen to your heart. Just keep pushing, and you will reach your destination. Don't give up - do what you love to do.

As I conclude my thoughts, I want to tell you "Picture AbhiBaki Hai Mere Dost" - Second inning is waiting to unfold.

I am writing my second half @40. When are you going to write your second half?

The J. J School of Employability Family

Akshay
Mahajan

Aloshree
Choudhury

Amrut
Bhadale

Bhavya
Hutasan

Dharmendra
Mohapatra

Chetan
Rohtagi

Deepika
Kumar

Jagdeep
Rana

Ifthekar

Jitendra Nath
Mahato

Keshava
Prasad

Lakshminarayanan
Jagannathan

Manidip
Ganguly

Manish
Makhijani

Mohammad
Zeeshan Ali

Narendra
Singh

Naveen
Gurusiddaiah

Praveen
Sah

Puneet
Mahajan

Rajesh
Ramamurthy

Ramnath
Kashikar

Riten
R. Rathod

S Vignesh

Sachin Amit

Sanjay
Dhumal

Smiley
Swaptosh

Sourav
Mondal

Srinivasa
Karthikeyan

Swagat Swagse
Pattnaik

Sudarshan
Gopal

T shankerdev

Varun Dutt

Vijaya Lakshmi